The
California
Trail
Yesterday & Today

The
California
Trail

Yesterday & Today

A Pictorial Journey
Along the California Trail

William E. Hill

Tamarack Books, Inc.

Second Edition

1 2 3 4 5 6 7 8 9 10

The California Trail Yesterday & Today was first published in 1986 by Pruett Publishing Company, Boulder, Colorado. They have graciously granted permission for this revised reprint.

Book cover and design by Kathleen Petersen

Typesetting by Typography by Gail Ward

Printed and bound in the United States of America

Tamarack Books, Inc.
PO Box 190313
Boise, ID 83719-0313
1-800-962-6657

Dedication

To those who've gone before

To those met along the way

and to those yet to follow

Contents

Foreword

The California gold rush was an epic event, a sudden and irradiating explosion of energy by the American people. Before 1849 the bold democratic experiment—something unique in the annals of mankind—had been largely confined to lands east of the Mississippi River; the lands west thereof were generally understood to be hostile and uninhabitable. Acquisition of California, after the war with Mexico, caused no stampede. What caused it was the electrifying news of gold at Sutter's Mill, and the resultant gold fever that afflicted over two million Americans.

To reach distant California roughly half of these adventurers went by sea, either around Cape Horn or via land links across Panama or Mexico. The other half traveled by land. There was just one land route that had the virtue of being centrally located and heading straight west—the great Platte River Road that led to South Pass, providential gateway through the Rocky Mountain barrier. While the seafarers also helped to populate California, the overland emigrants with their ox- or mule-powered covered wagons performed the additional feat of breaking the wilderness barrier, thus making possible the transformation of the United States into a truly trans-continental Union.

William Hill's book is about these landlubber argonauts and their incredible two thousand mile journey from jumping-off points along the Missouri River, across the dangerous wilder-ness of prairies, plains, deserts, and mountains to their ultimate destination, California. His book is designed for casual readers who may be content with a bird's-eye view of the overland experience, with samplings from the rich source materials. He has his facts commendably straight, and recommends other authoritative books for those inspired to explore the subject in greater depth. Of exceptional interest are selected contemporary maps and the illustrations of three rare and gifted trail artists. The author himself supplies excellent photographs of trail scenes today, taken on field trips to retrace the route to California and relive in imagination the golden odyssey of the Forty-niners.

The California Trail Yesterday and Today is a timely and welcome addition to a rapidly growing body of literature, both popular and scholarly, on a subject of perennial fascination. For all our revolutionary technical advances that compress time and space—so that we might, for example, travel from Missouri to California in three hours instead of the several months it took in 1849—we still stand in awe of the pioneers who, with nothing but their faith, courage, and primitive technology, blazed the trails and laid the foundations of modern America. ■

Merrill J. Mattes
Littleton, Colorado

Preface

California has lured people for more than one hundred fifty years. For some it has been a place to start a new life and to raise a family, while for others it has been a place to find or make a fortune to bring back to their family or to use for themselves. For me the lure hasn't been California itself, but the route to California that these early dreamers and adventurers took.

I can remember as a boy standing in front of a sign by the road describing the terrible hardships experienced on the Forty-Mile Desert and wondering how the emigrants ever made it. About twenty years ago on a return trip from California I came across another sign different from the one I remembered as a boy, but still about the Forty-Mile Desert. Reading it helped rekindle my interest in the trails west and the emigrants that took them. As a history teacher I had a professional interest and curiosity that became the motivating force behind my many journeys along the various trails since that trip. I hoped I could come to understand not only the hardships but also the feelings these early emigrants and gold-seeking "argonauts" experienced about one hundred fifty years ago as they traveled west on the trails.

For the past twenty years I have spent much of my spare time reading the diaries and journals of emigrants and the various guidebooks which became available to them as the years passed and the trails developed. I have also spent many hours looking at the drawings and sketches made by the emigrants on their westward treks. Parts of my summers were then spent locating the various sites that were mentioned or drawn by the emigrants in their diaries. I hoped that by finding and writing about them I could help in my own way to preserve their experiences so they would be available for others in the future.

In recent years two important movements have occurred that have helped save our trails west for future generations. First, there was the formation of new organizations to preserve the trails. The most recent and largest of these is called the Oregon-California Trails Association (OCTA, Box 1019, 524 S. Osage St., Independence, MO 64051–0519). It has as its major goal the identification, preservation, marking, and improved interpretation of the emigrant trails and related historical sites. This organization is proving to be both an effective and educational organization, attracting the attention and participation of both interested laymen and scholars alike. It has successfully marked large sections of the trails and numerous sites and has helped protect sections of the trails from being destroyed by new roads, pipelines, mining, and urban encroachment. Two other organizations, which predate it by a decade, are Trails West, Inc. and the Nevada Emigrant Trails Marking Committee of the Nevada Historical Society; both are dedicated to identifying and preserving the old trails and have done an outstanding job.

The other important development has been the renewed interest by the state and federal governments in protecting our heritage. Congress has recently expanded the National Historic Trails System to include the Oregon Trail, the Santa Fe Trail, and most recently, the California Trail and the Pony Express

Trail. Thus, the federal government is now committed by specific legislation to recognizing the importance and preserving these old highways, as well as the few forts and landmarks already preserved by the Department of the Interior and the National Park Service. In addition to the fine job already being done by the National Park Service, the Bureau of Land Management (BLM) has also taken a more active role in identifying, interpreting, and preserving the historic trails on the lands under its jurisdiction.

For future tourists and scholars of the west, these two developments will help preserve for them the way west that our earlier relatives and countrymen took. Furthermore, in the years ahead it will now be possible for many travelers to experience something of what the trek was like.

This book will introduce you to the California Trail and the emigrant experience. Other books go into much greater detail about the events and the people, but this one will let you "sample" the trail—to hear, see and feel what the way west was like.

Oh, don't you remember Sweet Betsey from Pike,
Who cross'd the big mountains with her lover Ike,
With two yoke of cattle, a large yellow dog,
A tall Shanghai rooster and one spotted hog.

Chorus:
Sing— too- ral- i, oo- ral- i, oo- ral- i- ay,
Sing— too- ral- i, oo- ral- i, oo- ral- i- ay.

They soon reached the desert, where Betsey gave out,
And down in the sand she lay rolling about;
While Ike, half-distracted, looked on with surprise,
Saying, "Betsey, get up, you'll get sand in your eyes."
Chorus.

Their wagon broke down with a terrible crash,
And out on the prairie rolled all kinds of trash;
A few little baby clothes done up with care—
'Twas rather suspicious, though all on the square.
Chorus.

The Shanghai ran off, and their cattle all died;
That morning the last piece of bacon was fried;
Poor Ike was discouraged, and Betsey got mad;
The dog drooped his tail and looked wondrously sad.
Chorus.

Sweet Betsey got up in a great deal of pain,
Declared she'd go back to Pike County again;
But Ike gave a sigh and they fondly embraced,
And they travelled along with his arm round her waist.
Chorus.

They suddenly stopped on a very high hill,
With wonder looked down upon old Placerville;
Ike sighed when he said, and he cast his eyes down,
"Sweet Betsey, my darling, we've got to Hangtown."
Chorus.

In this popular song of the California emigrants, there can be found much of what the trek to California was like. The song was both humorous and serious, describing both the emigrants themselves and the hardships experienced on their two thousand-mile journey to their "El Dorado," or for Betsey and Ike, "Hangtown" as Placerville was often called.

Between 1841 and 1860, about two hundred thousand emigrants trod the trail to California. They were hardy individuals with a dream of a better life, full of adventure, and a drive for self-preservation. They were resourceful when they needed to be and thankful when their trek was over.

Their journey was long and tiresome. The first half was usually the easiest, but the second half proved to be the more difficult—there came the mountains, then the deserts, then more mountains, and finally their goal, California! First would come the sun and the heat, then the lack of water and the sand. For the latecoming emigrants or stragglers, it could also be the winter snows and the cold. Breakdowns and the loss of materials either by accident or by necessity to lighten their loads caused many a hardship. With the exhaustion of food supplies, despair often set in, but if these could be overcome, their "El Dorado" could still be reached.

This book is a brief history of the early California Trail and a pictorial journey along it through the eyes and pens of the early emigrants along with photographs of the corresponding areas today.

Come join the author and "Betsey and Ike" on a journey west like you've never taken before. ∎

Acknowledgments

As with any other work, many people have helped by providing encouraging words, critical reviews, directions and information on the trail, and cooperation at various libraries and historical societies. While many could easily be noted, thanks must be given to those special few who most deserve it because they best represent those who assisted.

Over the years many ranchers were encountered, and almost all allowed me to walk around and drive through their properties. Many, like the Stevensons and the Bucks, however, took not just minutes, but hours and parts of working days to talk about the local history, the trail, its location, artifacts found, and anything they thought might be either interesting or helpful.

While some libraries and photographic divisions need better coordination, most libraries and historical societies were very cooperative. Linda Wickert, the Fine Arts Curator at the California Historical Society was very cooperative and went the "extra mile" when she easily could have done otherwise.

Many park superintendents, such as Wayne Brandt at Rock Creek and Jerry Banta at Scotts Bluff, should be singled out for their pride in their work and cooperation when providing access and information.

Certain individuals on a personal level gave me that extra spark. Helen Henderson's simple but encouraging words of "Do it!" when I was hesitant and first thinking about writing about the emigrant trails provided the boost I needed to get started. My parents, brothers, and sisters' constant inquiries about my progress kept me going. My father, Frederick W. Hill, and son, Will Hill, at times were my partners while driving along many of the desolate sections of the trails. They provided someone to talk with, to test out ideas, and to help as needed. ■

Introduction

The route to California and the California Trail are not synonymous. While the focus of this book will be the main overland route to California, there were other ways of getting to California that also deserve to be discussed because during certain years they were used more heavily than the main overland route.

First, however, let's examine the general route of the main California Trail. The eastern half of the trail coincided with that of the Oregon Trail. Its origins were the different "jumping-off" or embarking places along the Missouri River. Over the years the major embarking areas changed. Starting in 1841 it would have been Independence, Missouri, but soon other cities such as Westport, Fort Leavenworth, Weston, St. Joseph, Old Fort Kearny/Nebraska City, and Kanesville or the Council Bluffs area became the centers. The name of the particular route used by emigrants usually derived from the city of its origin—such as the Independence Road or the St. Joe Road. Because of the heavy use by the Mormons in the area around Kanesville or

Council Bluffs, the trail starting there and following the north side of the Platte River is sometimes called the Mormon Trail. It should be noted that it was used earlier by trappers, and later also by thousands of non-Mormon emigrants. In fact, research by one historian suggests that at least one-third of all central overland emigrants used this northern route, also known as the Council Bluffs Road. All these starting routes soon combined to form one main braid near Grand Island, Nebraska just east of where Fort Kearny was built.

Here at the confluence of the different routes, the emigrants traveled on both sides of the Platte River and then along the North Platte River. Near Casper, Wyoming, the emigrants left the North Platte and cut over to the Sweetwater River. Over the years of emigration many parallel routes were developed. Although they might weave a little from year to year, they all followed the "corridor" formed by these three river valleys and all were headed for and funneled through the great South Pass.

Once through the pass, the California emigrants and argonauts again had a choice of routes, depending on the year they traveled the trail. Some continued on the Oregon Trail to Fort Bridger and then north to Fort Hall and west along the Snake River until they cut off the Oregon Trail in the vicinity of the Raft River and crossed over to the Humboldt or Mary's River. Others would cut off the dip to Fort Bridger by using the Greenwood or Sublette Cutoff or many of the minor ones that soon developed in that region and then head for Fort Hall. Still others would later try the Hudspeth or Myers Cutoff before reaching Fort Hall. Some even went to Fort Bridger and then tried the Hastings Cutoff or followed the Mormon or Salt Lake route to the Humboldt. By 1859 the emigrants even had another route to use—the Lander Road. It cut off before South Pass at the Burnt Ranch and ended up near Fort Hall. No matter which route the emigrants used, they all finally ended up somewhere along the Mary's or Humboldt River in Nevada.

As on the eastern half of the trail, the emigrants were again funneled along a river, and a maze of trails developed along the Humboldt. Most emigrants followed it until the river "gave out" in the area known as "Humboldt Sink." But as with earlier sections of the trail, various routes were soon developed that offered the emigrants a choice of routes for the last segment of their journey, depending again on the year of the emigration. The three major ones were the Truckee, the Carson, and the Lassen routes, which terminated near Sutter's Fort and the "Gold Fields." Soon even these had their splinter routes, and many of them will be identified later in the history section of this book.

Many emigrants used other routes. Some turned southward from Salt Lake City to meet and follow the Old Spanish Trail (originating in Santa Fe) that led to Los Angeles. Still others started their journey to California by taking one of the southern routes that started in Texas. Others went southwestward from Santa Fe to get on the Gila River route to Los Angeles. In 1849, James Wilkins was on his way to California along the Platte when he met some wagons coming east. After inquiring they told him they were returning to take the Santa Fe Trail because they were afraid that with all the emigrants ahead of them on the main trail there would not be enough grass left for their own stock. Some emigrants tried a new cutoff from the Salt Lake-Los Angeles Road and went through an area that came to be called "Death Valley" because of all the suffering that faced the emigrants there. Briefly then, these were some of the other overland routes that were used by some of the emigrants.

The following statistics taken from John Unruh's *The Plains Across*, University of Illinois Press, show the number of emigrants by year that came to California by the overland route:

1841	34	1848	400	1855	1,500
1842	0	1849	25,000	1856	8,000
1843	38	1850	44,000	1857	4,000
1844	53	1851	1,100	1858	6,000
1845	260	1852	50,000	1859	17,000
1846	1,500	1853	20,000	1860	9,000
1847	450	1854	12,000		

Thus, it seems that about two hundred thousand emigrants went overland to California, and another one hundred thousand went to Oregon and Utah during this same twenty-year period.

In addition to the overland routes there were still other ways to California, which during some years proved to be more popular with the emigrants and argonauts. These were the sea routes. By booking passage on a sailing ship or steamer one of several routes could be used. The most popular was the all-water route around Cape Horn totaling about thirteen thousand nautical miles. The others were also by water, but with intermediate land crossings of Panama, Nicaragua, or Mexico. The longest, the Panama route, was over five thousand miles. These routes had been used by the Spanish merchants and navy since colonial days to get to California, but it was the US interest in California and then the discovery of gold that brought about the fuller development of these routes, especially the Panama route.

Because of the popularity of the sea routes with many of the California argonauts during the gold rush period, an examination and comparison of them with the overland route with their respective problems should be considered.

The emigrants who used the overland route as opposed to the sea route tended to come from different areas and socioeconomic groups. Generally the sea routes were more expensive than the overland route. The per passenger cost started at about $150 but averaged about $300 for the trip around the Horn. The total cost of the trip by way of Panama was about $455, but during the gold rush years tickets were frequently sold by "scalpers" for three times as much or more, and they were readily purchased. This cost included not only the passage but also the food during the voyage. Because of the higher costs, the sea route tended to be used by wealthier people such as doctors, lawyers, businessmen, and other professionals. The passengers also tended to come from the coastal and urban areas, especially the northeast with New York City as the main port. For the average rural family, the total cost was prohibitive, yet a single person might use it.

The overland route was largely taken by the interior or rural families and tended to have a lower per capita cost. It is true that many professional people traveled on the trails, but they tended to come from the interior lands. The many single men who went overland during the gold rush frequently signed on with a wagon company and paid from $50.00 to $150.00 depending on the work arrangements made with the leader. The typical farm family averaged between four to six people and traveled by wagon. It is a little more difficult to figure costs for the overland route, but by using various guidebooks a good basis can be found. Depending on the specific type and number of draft animals used—oxen, mules, or horses—total costs can be given. Ware's 1849 guidebook put the total cost of wagon, teams, and supplies at $600.00 for ox teams and $670.78 for mule teams. Street's 1851 guidebook listed the estimated cost at $522.16 for ox teams and $600.00 for mule teams. By 1859 Marcy's guide listed $409.00 for an ox team and $809.00 for a mule team. Thus, by using the average number of emigrants, and the cost for wagon and team, it seems that the cost of individual transportation was between $100 and $200. Hopefully the emigrant still had some stock and their wagon when they arrived in California, and this reduced their net cost even more. The wagon itself was a small farm or spring wagon, which cost between $80.00 to $85.00 while the cover or canvas might cost as much as $100.00.

Each year as more improvements were made along the trail, miscellaneous expenses for ferries and tolls tended to increase. Typical charges for ferries and bridges averaged from $3.00 to $6.00 per wagon and from twenty-five to fifty cents per animal. Yet, the actual charge varied greatly depending on what the operator thought they could extract from the emigrant. Some small bridges charged twenty-five cents per wagon while the most expensive was recorded at $16.00 at one Green River ferry. One emigrant put their extra expenses at $75.00, but suggested a family bring $150.00 to be sure.

There were perhaps three major advantages for the emigrants traveling by ship. First, they could leave at just about anytime of the year as long as voyages were scheduled. The most difficult part of the voyage was rounding the Horn, and it could be especially hard if the trip occurred during the Southern Hemisphere's winter months of July and August. The overland emigrants were restricted as far as when they could leave their jumping-off places because they could only leave late in spring when there were sufficient prairie grasses to sustain their livestock. If they left too early the grasses would not be out and their livestock would starve; in leaving too late there would be difficulty finding grass because earlier companies' stock had grazed the grasses away. Also if they left too late or traveled too slowly, they chanced getting caught in the mountains during the winter snows as the Donner party did in 1846. Therefore, most wagon companies left within four to six weeks of each other from April to May and were rarely out of contact or sight of other wagon companies, especially during the years of heavy overland traffic.

The second advantage of going by sea was that the emigrants could carry more supplies and equipment if they desired and wished to pay for it. The overland emigrant was limited by the size of their wagon and the number of people sharing it. The average number of people per wagon was four, depending on the year of emigration. Most of the early emigrants brought only one wagon and were lucky if they still had it when they arrived in California. By the early to mid 1850s, emigrant families often recorded the provision of a second or perhaps a third vehicle for their trip. Other factors that ultimately played significant roles were the pretrip planning and the strength of their draft animals and their ability to last during the journey. Many an emigrant had to jettison some or all of their belongings before their journey was completed. A reporter for a St. Louis paper at Fort Kearny wrote that "soon it was found that the loading was too great for the teams, and now overboard goes everything. The road is lined with various articles—even gold vases and gold washers." Wilkins noted this about the Platte, "The road all along is strewed with old clothes boots provisions, particularly beans, I notice are left, and the wreck of wagons." At Fort Laramie he wrote that "a great many parties abandoning their wagons at this point and take to mule packing on account of rumours of no grass and bad rocky roads." Those who packed could carry even less than those with wagons. For those emigrants who kept their wagons many would finally be abandoned at the desert when their animals gave out.

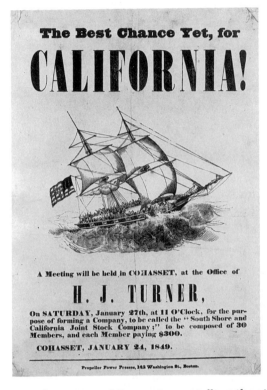

CALIFORNIA!
*Courtesy, Bostonian Society,
Old State House*

This is one of the posters extolling the virtues of both the ship and the voyage by sea to California and the gold fields.

There was a third advantage for those emigrants who decided to cross the Isthmus of Panama and that was time. The trip at its fastest could take between one to two months, depending on the year the journey was made. In Street's guidebook of 1851, he listed the approximate time as forty-five days by steamer. It was the completion of the railroad across

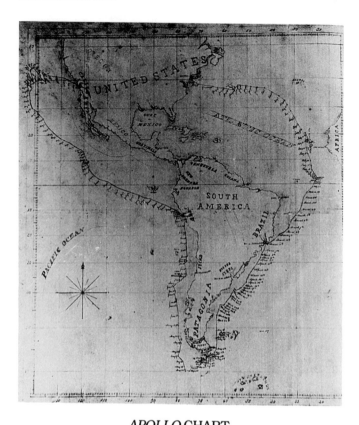

APOLLO CHART
Courtesy, National Maritime Museum

The map above shows the crossing of the Isthmus of Panama as drawn by George P. Clark in 1850. The route involved boat travel up the Chagres River and then overland by mule to the Pacific and hopefully another ship.

Panama by Wills Aspenwall by 1855 that drastically reduced the travel time from days to a few hours. The record for the route by way of Panama was twenty-one days in 1855. The trip around the Horn usually took less time than the overland journey, but some like the ship *Apollo* took as long as nine months, while the overland journey normally took between five and seven months. The record in 1849 was set by the *Greyhound*, one of the new clipper-type ships, which made it in 112 days. In 1853 the *Northern Light* returned to New York from San Francisco in only seventy-six days. These were more the exception than the rule. By the early 1850s the average time for a clipper ship was about 132 days. Yet, as improvements were made all along the trail, overland travel became faster and faster. In little more than a decade the time was nearly cut in half, and the route around the Horn began to lose its time advantage.

However, there were many problems that faced the ocean-going argonauts. Some were very similar to those experienced by the overland emigrants, but others were different.

Disease was one of the major problems that faced both the overland emigrants and those that went by sea. Cholera was the major killer on the California Trail during the years 1849, 1850, and 1852, taking an estimated two thousand or more lives each year. The disease also was contracted by those who came by sea. In 1849 people in Panama City were afflicted with it; it had come in with the gold seekers who then carried it to San Francisco. On his return voyage in 1852, Byron McKinstry noted that twelve deaths due to cholera occurred during the nine-day trip between Panama and New York. The people aboard ship could not keep separate from those with the disease or leave the ship. In 1855 one ship with 650 passengers lost 113 to cholera. Nevertheless the disease never came close to killing the number of people aboard ship that it did on the overland route during the cholera outbreak's worst years. In fact, one estimate by Donald Jackson in his book *Gold Dust* put the total deaths at around fifty for all the sea voyages for 1849. More may have died in the cities, such as Panama City, however.

Smallpox was another feared disease and killer of emigrants on both land and sea. Other diseases such as yellow fever and malaria were especially dangerous for those crossing the Isthmus of Panama. In 1851 Borthwick crossed Panama, and he wrote that "there was here at this time a great deal of sickness, and absolute misery, among the Americans. Diarrhea and fever were the prevalent diseases."

One unique malady of the seagoing emigrants was sea-sickness, and it was the most common illness of all. It struck most passengers, especially at the outset of their journey. In

1852 Charles Harvey's first diary entry stated that the ship sailed from New York with "loud cheers" and "booming of cannons." The very next day, March 3, he noted that he "felt poorly eat verry little . . . good many passengers sick." Finally on March 8 he wrote, "Felt little better, eat little grewel." Even John Beach, son of the owner of the ship *Apollo* suffered from it when only four days out of New York. Most people finally got accustomed to the normal rolling of the ship, and some passengers even likened it to the rolling of a wagon on the prairie.

Weather was a problem for all the emigrants. On the sea, storms could increase the amount and severity of seasickness, but they could also be more troublesome. The storms at the Horn often caused ships, like the *Henry Lee* to take as long as forty days to round it. Passengers often lashed themselves to their berths during bad weather. They were constantly soaked and hot food of any kind was impossible. JD Borthwick said during one gale "that boxes and chests of all sizes, besides casks of provisions and other ship's stores, which had got adrift, were cruising about promiscuously . . . . In the morning we found the cook's galley had fetched away, and the stove was rendered useless." That wasn't the only problem with winds and storms. In 1852 the *Grecian* lost her mizzen and fore topmast in a gale. In 1857 the ship *Central America* sank and about 400 passengers were lost. Sometimes ships, such as the *Union* and *John A. Sutter* ran aground.

At other times ships were forced to wait for a "fair wind." Charles Harvey's whole entry for one day was, "Dead calm," and on another, "Quite warm, The wind died away this morning and we are becalmed again water getting short provisions poor and a hot sun which makes it verry unpleasant and discourageing." The *Elizabeth* was becalmed in the extreme cold of Patagonia for nearly three weeks, and the *Apollo* waited almost two weeks west of San Francisco for a fair wind to take her into port.

For the overland emigrants the unpredictable prairie storms could bring torrential rains in minutes, which could flood rivers and back up river crossings for days, make the trail muddy or "heavy," or even flood them out. In 1850 George Keller reached the Ham's Fork but "found impossible to ford, on account of its swollen state." It took three days before they crossed and three attempts to construct a ferry strong enough. On the evening of June 13, 1853, James Woodworth had camped in a hollow for the evening. He wrote that the "wind bleu with great violence At the same time a terrible storm of rain accompanied with hard thunder came on . . . [the hollow] it soon filled to a depth of Six inches with water and all of the bedcloths were swimming in it We of course were obliged to evacuate the tent without ceremony and pass the night as best we could."

Just as the overland emigrants had problems with food, passengers aboard ship frequently complained about both the quantity and quality of food and the foul-tasting water from the ship's caskets. On one voyage passengers complained that "there were two bugs for every bean" with their meals, but adding humorously that at least they had some fresh meat with their meals. By the end of the voyage they were frequently down to salt meat, beans, and hardtack. Mores Cogswell, a passenger bound for California on the *Sweden* wrote that "the beans are 3 to a quart of hot water, with a small piece of rusty pork." In 1860 Henry Huston on the steamer *Sonora* commented that some of the food was "'old enough to vote,' then 'roast beef' with a brown crust and all inside raw and bloody." The fish "all well rotted; Bread, Fruit and other solids come in about the same shape; Butter is here a liquid; tea and coffee are both nick-names, as those liquids very seldom have a taste of those vegetable, for which they are named." Water was often rationed and passengers on the *Grecian* complained about the rationing of water by the cupful.

On the overland trail food supplies were also down to a minimum by the time they reached the Humboldt and Carson sinks. James Wilkins wrote of the Pioneer Line, the first commercial wagon train to cross the plains, that "they like us had nothing left but bread and bacon." Finding freshwater supplies was also a problem because the springs and streams were frequently contaminated by human and animal wastes and

ISTHMUS OF PANAMA CROSSING
Courtesy, New York Historical Society

This chart shows the 1849 voyage of the ship *Apollo* which lasted about nine months. The trip "around the Horn" was very popular with the forty-niners. The voyage was about 13,000 nautical miles. Each day's position was noted on the chart, and its progress or lack of it can be seen.

dead carcasses. Further, on certain parts of the trail, such as the Sublette Cutoff, Salt Lake Desert, Black Rock Desert, and Forty-Mile Desert, good water was between forty to eighty miles away.

One disease usually associated with the sea voyages was scurvy. While records do indicate that some died, they do not indicate that the problem was as severe as many first feared. It was, however, another problem that hit the overland emigrants. Wilkins wrote on September 19, 1849, "We are most of us taking the scurvey, myself amongst the rest, the gums bleed and the skin is becoming discoloured in patches." DT McCollum, another emigrant on the trail, noted that "nearly half the passengers in the Pioneer Line . . . have had the Scurvy, and four have died with it." Bruff wrote on September 30, 1849, "Much scurvy among the emigrants, a little girl's mouth badly affected with it." These accounts were expressed late in the journey of the emigrants. In 1850, however, George Keller did state that people were suffering from scurvy at Fort Laramie, which was much further east on the trail.

For the ocean voyagers there was not much in the way of sightseeing nor even the change of scenery, and boredom became a major problem. Yet, some well-organized groups were prepared. One from New York brought along a 150-volume library to read on their voyage. There probably wasn't much left of it once they arrived in San Francisco. On another ship Charles Harvey recorded that he passed much of his time by reading, playing euchre, jackstraws, hunting lice, and carving canes and rings. While some ships, such as the *Sweden,* sailed without stopping, most made one or two stops. On the Atlantic the ports were usually Rio de Janeiro or Santa Catarina and on the Pacific, Talcahuano or Valparaiso. Brief as the stops were, the passengers made the most of them. On the other hand, overland travelers frequently commented on the landscape and many took time to "sightsee" by looking at a gorge, or strange mound, or climbing rocks and carving their names on them.

While emigrants on the overland route had trouble finding camping grounds with sufficient grass and water, they at least could sleep in the "wide open spaces." Passengers on ship were often overcrowded. The average size of a sailing ship in 1849 carried forty-eight argonauts plus crew and was ninety-three feet long and twenty-four feet abeam. This did not leave much room to roam. By the 1850s, the new larger clipper ships could carry about three hundred passengers, but space was still tight.

OLD SAN FRANCISCO HARBOR
Smithsonian Institution Photo #38416-C

Here is San Francisco harbor literally jammed with vessels. Many of them were abandoned by their crews and left to rot while the crews took off for the gold diggings.

The early steamers could carry about two hundred passengers while by the late 1850s and early 1860s, some carried seven hundred, but still space was scarce. The first steamer from Panama City, the *California*, was forced to take on board 365 passengers while it was built for only 215 after the gold seekers had threatened the captain. Even on regular voyages sleeping quarters were crowded. Sleeping berths were often tiered—three abreast two feet apart one on top of the other. Passengers on the *Alexander Von Humboldt* were nine to a compartment—a six-foot square. One could only imagine what the aroma must have been like after months at sea or after stormy weather.

One last problem for the oceangoing emigrants was that there were fire and explosions on steamers. Although fire was a very rare occurrence, the ship *Independence* burned in 1853 and 125 out of 300 passengers died. For the overland emigrant their major problem with fire was getting enough wood, sage, or buffalo chips for their cooking fires. Often they would make use of a discarded wagon as a fuel supply. One has often heard of great prairie fires facing emigrants, and some did experience them, but there just aren't many records to substantiate them as a common problem. This is probably due to the fact that when the emigrants were on the plains it was spring and the grasses were short and green. By the time they were traveling during the drier months of summer, they were traveling in the desert or drier areas of the trail where there was little vegetation to burn.

These then were some of the difficult realities facing the oceangoing emigrants and their overland counterparts. Despite the problems, traveling by sea proved to be extremely popular after gold was discovered in 1848. San Francisco had welcomed only two US ships in 1848, but in 1849 over 775 ships brought the argonauts. More people came by ship in 1849 than came by wagon. The estimates range from a low of over 22,000 to a high of 40,000 emigrants by ship, while about 6,200 wagons moved between 21,000 and 23,000 emigrants to California. In the years that followed, both the sea and land routes continued to be popular and the population of California grew rapidly. ■

Early History
of the
California Trail

1818–21 The Mexican War for independence from Spain was started by Father Miguel Hidalgo y Costilla. Formal independence for Mexico was finally granted and signed in 1821.

1819 The Adams-Onis Treaty was signed with Spain. This set the northern boundary of the Mexican Territory as the forty-second parallel to the Continental Divide. The area directly north of it was the Oregon Territory and was claimed by the United States, Great Britain, and Russia. Russia still had an outpost in California, Fort Ross, which it had set up and dedicated on September 10, 1812. They would later sell it to John Sutter.

1821
After Mexican independence, US interests in California began to increase. At first it was a merchant venture with interests in shipping cattle hides and sea otter skins back east. Later Americans would come to the California area in hopes of starting a new life or finding gold.

1824
The South Pass was traversed by trappers including Jedediah Smith, Jim Bridger, Thomas Fitzpatrick, and James Clyman. Within a few decades, nearly all of the traffic heading west for Oregon, California, and Utah was funnelled through the broad flat pass.

Tom Fitzpatrick and other trappers are said to have camped at Independence Rock and celebrated the Fourth of July there. Some sources also credit Fitzpatrick with naming the rock. Other sources assert that William Sublette and his trappers gave the rock its name while celebrating Independence Day there in 1830. This large granite rock would become a major landmark on the overland trails to California and Oregon. Father DeSmet later called this rock the "Great Register of the Desert" because of all the names written and carved on it by those who visited it—both trapper and emigrant alike.

1826
Joseph Robidoux set up a trading post near the banks of the Missouri River. The site was to become the city of St. Joseph.

Jedediah Smith, the famous mountain man, led a party of trappers to California and the San Gabriel Mission. He was looking for new beaver grounds and also hoping to find the mythical San Buenaventura River, which would open the Rocky Mountains up to oceangoing ships. In entering Mexican California he broke the law, was put in jail, and then released on the promise that he would leave California by the same way he entered. He started to leave but then hunted and set up a stockade on the Stanislaus River. While some of his men remained he left for the Rendezvous at Bear Lake and returned to California when it was over. He was jailed and then released again on the promise to leave and not return. This time headed north to the Oregon Territory. Other trappers such as Sylvester Pattie had similar problems with the Mexican officials.

The route Smith used to enter California was not well documented, but there is little evidence that it was used by later emigrants. However, a river where they camped while going north did come to be known as the "American River," and this does become important in California's history.

1827 The town of Independence, Missouri, was founded.
It became the jumping-off place for the Santa Fe Trail and later the California and Oregon trails. The first wagon company left for California from Independence in 1841. Independence Square and the courthouse marked the beginning of the trails. It was the springs in the area that made Independence a natural location for both the town and the trails.

Fort Leavenworth was established by the military on the Missouri River. It provided protection for the Santa Fe Trail. During the years of the early gold rush in California it served as another of the jumping-off centers for the emigrants.

1828 Hiram Scott, a trapper, was left by his companions
and disappeared. The following year William Sublette found a skeleton that was believed to have been Scott's. The bluffs along that section of the Platte River were named for him. Over the years different stories developed about who Hiram Scott was and how he came to die. As early as 1830, the first written record of the legend was made by Warren Ferris.

1828-36 Andrew Jackson was elected president of the
United States, and he shortly began negotiations with Mexico to purchase California and New Mexico. After six years the negotiations broke off. Succeeding presidents continued to try to obtain California.

1833 John C. McCoy founded the town of Westport a few miles west of Independence. Once Westport Landing was developed on the Missouri, the two areas grew together and it also became another jumping-off place for the emigrant trail.

JOSEPH R. WALKER
*Courtesy, Joslyn Art Museum,
Omaha, NE*

Joseph Redderford Walker was possibly the most famous and successful of the mountain men. Walker helped Bonneville in the 1830s and Fremont in the 1840s. He was the first to really explore the Great Basin, even more than Jedediah Smith did. He opened up much of what became the California Trail, discovered the Walker Pass, and was the first white man in Yosemite Valley. In 1837, he was a guide for Sir William Drummond Stewart's famous hunting expedition to the Rockies and was painted by Alfred J. Miller. He helped guide many an emigrant to California.

1833-34 Joseph Walker, another famous trapper and mountain man, traveled from the Salt Lake region down the Mary's or Humboldt River. He crossed the Sierra Nevada down near their southern end at a pass that now bears his name, Walker Pass. While his whole route was not used by the emigrants, many traveled on certain parts of it. In 1869 the transcontinental railroad also used parts of it.

1834 Some believe that Kit Carson and other trappers were the pathfinders for the route down the Raft River to Goose Creek and over to Bishop's Creek, headwaters of the Mary's or Humboldt River. He then traveled part way down the Humboldt River along the same general route used earlier by Walker and then returned. Trappers now used this route to hunt beavers in the upper part of the Mary's River. This route later became the main branch of the California Trail from Fort Hall.

Fort William was constructed near the mouth of the Laramie River on the North Platte by Robert Campbell, William Sublette's co-partner. This fort was visited by Alfred J. Miller, painter for Sir William Drummond Stewart, in 1837, while he was on a "tour" of the American West. Miller's paintings of the fort are the only ones that exist of the fort and are well-known today. The fort changed owners many times during the next few years, and finally a new fort replaced it in 1841 just in time for the development of the California-Oregon trails.

Nathaniel J. Wyeth contracted to sell supplies at the Rendezvous, but by the time he arrived there others were already selling supplies to the mountain men. Wyeth decided to construct a fort on the Snake River and it was called Fort Hall. In 1837 it was sold to the Hudson's Bay Company, and they enlarged it from its original size to about eighty by one hundred and twenty feet. In 1856 the fort was abandoned, and by 1862 it had succumbed to the flooding of the Snake. The fort served as the last major resupply area for the California-bound emigrants who did not take the many cutoffs that developed earlier along the trail.

1836 The first California revolution for independence was led by native-born Californios, Juan Bautista Alvarado and Jose Castro. Alvarado's proclamation of independence on November 7, 1836, was supported by thirty U.S. and British frontiers-men. However, when the Mexican government appointed Alvarado the legitimate governor of California he ended the rebellion. In 1846 Castro was planning another rebellion against Mexico, but the American supported Bear Flag Revolt swept by him.

John Marsh arrived in California. He was an adventurer, trapper, storekeeper, former Indian agent, and finally major landowner in California. He left Missouri for California when threatened with arrest for selling guns illegally to the Indians. Once in California he set up a practice as a physician. Shortly thereafter he obtained a large ranch of about fifty thousand acres on San Francisco Bay. His ranch became one of the objectives for many of the later California emigrants. He also actively encouraged Americans to come to California.

1837
Joseph Moore founded the Missouri River town of Weston. For a few years in the 1850s, it rivaled Independence and St. Joseph as a jumping-off place. James Wilkins disembarked here in 1849. By 1860 Weston's boom period was over.

1839
John Sutter arrived in California. He originally left Switzerland to escape a jail sentence, came to the United States and then journeyed to Oregon in 1838, traveling with a party of missionaries. He went to California by way of Hawaii and Alaska. He was another adventurer like Marsh and soon became another large landowner. He persuaded Governor Alvarado to grant him eleven square miles of land, about forty-seven thousand acres, and finally obtained two more large land grants. He promised the governor to set up a colony of Swiss to serve as a buuffer between the Americans, British, Russians, and the Mexicans. His colony of "New Helvetia" was at the junction of the American and Sacramento rivers. There he built his fort which became the headquarters for his empire of the future— Sutter's Fort; it became the desired destination for Americans who came over the California Trail. Today Sutter's Fort has been restored and reconstructed and can be visited.

JOHN SUTTER
Courtesy, Sutter's Fort
State Historic Monument

His dream was to create his own empire. He was well on his way until the discovery of gold and the takeover of California by the United States. Both of these events caused Sutter more problems than benefits. Sutter's fate was like that of John McLoughlin's of Oregon— both men helped the early emigrants and both lost their empires and never completely recovered.

The two ranchos of John Marsh and John Sutter soon developed into the end of the trail for the pre-gold rush emigrants. They served as a resupply depot for the emigrants who succeeded in arriving in California and needed materials to start their new lives. For the early years of the trail they also served as a base station for rescue missions for emigrants needing help back on the trail. The parties that finally rescued the survivors of the Donner party left from Fort Sutter. Thus, for the California emigrants, these two ranches played a role similar to that played by the Lee and Whitman missions and Fort Vancouver for the Oregon emigrants.

John Bidwell, a member of the Western Emigration Society, tried to get people interested in traveling to California. His work, plus that by others such as John Marsh and the old trapper Robidoux, had stirred the interests of people in Missouri, Arkansas, Illinois, and Kentucky. By the winter of 1840, plans were made by many of them to meet in Independence by May 9, 1841, to start their trek to California.

1840
British and Americans at home and in California increased their agitation for a takeover of the Mexican state of California.

1841
The old wooden Fort William was abandoned and replaced by another structure made out of adobe and called Fort John. Most emigrants along the trail called it Fort Laramie as they did the earlier Fort William. Laramie Peak is the predominant geographical feature in that area and served as a landmark for travelers in that area. The new fort was about 123 feet by 168 feet. Francis Parkman, a young adventurer and writer stayed there in 1846 and gives one of the best descriptions of the fort itself. He stated that "the little fort is built of bricks dried in the sun . . . of oblong form, with bastions of clay . . . at two of the corners . . . . The walls are about fifteen feet high." This was a major stopping place for the emigrants and it signified the completion of the prairie portion of their journey.

The Russians voluntarily left Fort Ross and with it their interests in California. They had already agreed in 1824 not to expand their interests below fifty-four degrees, forty minutes north. John Sutter purchased the fort from the Russians and its role in California history was over. Fort Ross has also been restored and reconstructed and can be visited today.

This was the year the US emigrants began to arrive in California over what ultimately developed into the California Trail. There were three groups—one from Oregon, including women and children; another from New Mexico, following the caravan trail to Los Angeles; and the third, the Bidwell party. This latter group were the first emigrants to travel across the Sierra Nevada to John Marsh's ranch and then to Sutter's Fort along the general route that came to be known as the California Trail.

The party of emigrants met in May in Independence, Missouri, as had been previously decided. It was comprised of sixty-nine people. The company was called the Bartleson-Bidwell party. They luckily were able to join a party of missionaries, including the famous Father DeSmet who was being guided by Thomas Fitzpatrick and Joseph Meek. They followed what was to be called the Oregon-California Trail. West of Soda Springs the company divided. Thirty-four emigrants continued with the missionaries on the Oregon Trail to Fort Hall and then to Oregon, while thirty-five turned south to break open a route to California. While the complete route they took was not followed by later emigrants, parts of it were to be used. Nancy Kelsey and her baby, Ann, were the first woman and child on the California Trail. In Utah, they called one of their camping places Rabbit Spring, and it is still known by that name today. They faced great hardships crossing the Great Salt Lake Desert and finally after moving southwest found a pass, Harrison Pass, in the Ruby Mountains and crossed over to the Mary's or Humboldt River. They were forced to abandon their wagons before crossing the mountains and thus continued their journey by foot and pack animals. After following the Mary's River they continued south to the Walker River and crossed the Sierra Nevada at or near the Sonora Pass. These were the first emigrants, but because they left their wagons the first successful wagon company would have to wait a few more years. Also, the probable pass they used was not selected again by other emigrants until 1852.

1842   John Fremont, guided by Kit Carson, headed out from Westport to South Pass and the Rocky Mountains. With his cartographer, Charles Preuss, they mapped the trail and recorded information which became very useful to emigrants who used the route. A few years later they completed the route all the way to Oregon and published their reports, which were widely know and read in the late 1840s.

No emigrant wagon companies left for California in 1842, but companies left for Oregon and, thus, developed the first half of the trail. About twelve of the men who went west to California in 1841 returned to the States, trying to find a better route while also using part of their 1841 trail. They were led by Chiles and Hopper. Many of the members of this party became important to the history of California and the trail. Creeks, rivers, towns, lakes, mountains, and forts were named after these hardy emigrants. Many also became guides for later emigrant companies and helped to open new routes and will be noted later in this book.

President Tyler tried again to negotiate with Mexico to obtain California. However, his efforts failed when a brash Commodore Jones "captured" Monterey on October 19, thinking war with Mexico had broken out. As a result the Mexicans became even more suspicious of the United States.

1842–43 Jim Bridger and Louis Vasquez built a
trading post near the Black's Fork of the Green River. It was on the bluffs but was later moved to the bottomland. This trading post became a major stopping and resupply area for the early emigrants and for the later ones who used the Salt Lake Road or cutoff to California. For those emigrants who took any of the different cutoffs, such as the Greenwood or Sublette, Slate Creek, Kinney, Baker-Davis, or Lander Road, the fort was by-passed. Brigham Young purchased the fort or post in 1855, but it was abandoned and burned in 1857. The US Army constructed a new fort on the old location almost immediately. Today parts of the old military fort have been restored. A replica of Bridger's fort has also been built near its original site. The fort is a state historic site and is a living museum.

1843 St. Joseph, Missouri, was laid out on the site of the
earlier trading post. It soon developed into another of the major embarking areas for the westward emigrants. It also became the eastern terminus of the short-lived Pony Express in 1860.

Joseph Chiles organized a wagon company to return with him to California. Even though he had not succeeded with wagons in 1841, he decided to try again with them. The party included about eight wagons and thirty people—many were friends and relatives, including women and children of people already in California. His wagon company traveled behind the "Great Migration" of the emigrants to Oregon and also behind John C. Fremont who was on another of his trips of exploration to Oregon. His return to the States from Oregon would bring Fremont through California. Chiles's party followed the already defined route of the Oregon Trail as it was called then, all the way to Fort Hall. There he decided to divide the company. Joseph Walker led the largest group with the women and children and the wagons, while Chiles took some of the men and led a pack train on a different route. Walker turned off the Oregon Trail at Calder Creek, cut over to the Raft River, then to the City of the Rocks, and down to the Mary's River. The original plan called for Walker to meet Chiles near the Humboldt Sink after he had successfully entered California from the north and found a new route across the Sierra Nevada. However, Chiles wasn't there and Walker headed south along the route he had taken back in 1834. About five hundred miles of the route Walker established, from the Raft River to the Humboldt Sink, became the major route of the California Trail. As for Chiles, his route had continued west along the Oregon Trail until finally reaching Fort Boise. A little west of there he cut southwest finally picking up the Sacramento River and more or less followed it to Sutter's Fort. This route proved to be as poor as the other. Walker's party had been forced to abandon their wagons near Owens Lake, and thus, it would take another year before wagons would make it all the way across the Sierra Nevada and into California.

1844 This year Fremont completed his exploration and mapping of the route to Oregon that he had begun in 1842. Fremont decided to return to the United States by heading south into California. By February he made it to Sutter's Fort. This venture into Mexican territory by members of the US Army

made Mexico nervous. Fremont claimed he needed fresh horses for his journey to cross the Sierra Nevada. He then returned to the United States, mapping his route all the way. While this route was not used by the emigrants, his maps showed that the lands between the Rocky and Sierra Nevada formed a "Great Basin." He would return again to California in 1845, giving names to a number of places and changing the Mary's River named earlier by Peter Skene Ogden of the Hudson's Bay Company to the Humboldt River. The Carson River was named for his scout, Kit Carson, and the entrance to San Francisco was later named the "Golden Gate."

Peter Lassen, a Dane, obtained a land grant from the Mexican government about one hundred miles north of Sutter's Fort on the Sacramento River. Lassen had come to California by way of Oregon in 1839–40 and had hoped to create an empire like Sutter's and to get rich off the new emigrants. His chance would come in a few years.

This was the year that the first wagon company made it over the Sierra Nevada, establishing at last a usable wagon route. It was led by Elisha Stephens who served as captain. The Stephens-Townsend-Murphy party, as it is often called, set off from Council Bluffs, Iowa, in March 1844. It was comprised of twenty-three men, eight women, and fifteen children. Caleb Greenwood and his sons acted as pilots for the first half of the trail. It followed the established Oregon Trail as far as South Pass. Shortly thereafter they decided to try a new cutoff. Isaac "Old Man" Hitchcock suggested that they cut west instead of heading southwest to Fort Bridger and thereby save some time. It seemed that Hitchcock knew generally of the route and that it may have been used by Bonneville in 1832 but not since then. The company discussed it and voted to try it. While it proved drier and longer than originally thought, all made it safely across. In fact, part of the company returned back over the route to the Big Sandy to look for cattle that had been lost and then returned to cross it again. This route came to be called the Greenwood Cutoff and, later, the Sublette Cutoff.

ELISHA STEPHENS
Courtesy, Clyde Arbuckle
Collection, San Jose, CA

Elisha Stephens was another mountain man and guide. In 1844, he led the first successful wagon train over the Sierra Nevada into California over the Truckee Route and through what is now called Donner Pass. This is the only known photograph of Stephens. It was taken twenty years after he led the emigrants over the mountains.

After crossing the Bear Mountains they headed north toward Fort Hall. Shortly after leaving Fort Hall they cut across and followed Walker's route all the way down the Humboldt. At the Humboldt Sink and the "Forty-Mile Desert," as it is called later, they came in contact with an Indian called Truckee. He told them of a stream and passage west across the desert. They crossed over to it and followed it up into the mountains. Today the river still bears the name given it by the thankful emigrants as does a meadow area, respectively the Truckee River and Truckee Meadows, the present site of Reno. From there the emigrants crossed at what is now called Donner's Pass and Donner Creek down the west side of the mountains. While they were forced to temporarily leave their wagons at various places along the trail and some of the emigrants were even forced to spend part of the winter in cabins they built, they all arrived safely by the spring of 1845. In addition to the first use of the Greenwood Cutoff and the bringing of the first wagons to California, two children were born along the way: Ellen Independence Miller near Independence Rock and Elizabeth Yuba Murphy near Yuba Creek.

Lansford Hastings left California by sea for the east, hoping to encourage emigration to California and to publish a guidebook. His guidebook would contain the infamous Hastings Cutoff, the route taken by the ill-fated Donner party in 1846, but only vaguely described and never traveled by Hastings. He had originally gone to Oregon in 1842 and then left after not finding what he had hoped for and decided that California was the better place to make his fortune.

1845 James K. Polk became president and pledged

himself to obtain California for the United States. His plan was three-pronged. First, he hoped to obtain it by direct negotiations and purchase. Second, he encouraged independence movements in California by pledging to protect any Americans seeking to make California part of the United States. As a result, Secretary of State Buchanan instructed Consul Larkin to "arouse in their bosoms that love of liberty and independence so natural to the American continent," and that "if the People should desire to unite their destiny with ours, they would be received as brethren." Polk's third plan was war if all else failed.

More emigrants and wagon companies headed west, but most still were bound for Oregon. St. Joseph was the major embarking area. Caleb Greenwood and his sons returned from Sutter's Fort back over the California Trail to meet the Oregon-bound emigrants. They were to encourage them to head for California instead of Oregon. At this they proved to be immensely successful. Over fifty wagons and more than 250 emigrants, including women and children, turned away from Oregon near the Raft River and headed for California. This was five times as many people and wagons than that which had made the first successful journey in 1844. William B. Ide and his family were one of the families that traveled to California. He along with other emigrants of 1845 would play a major role in the 1846 Bear Flag Revolt for independence.

Lansford Hastings headed for California, but he traveled by horse not wagon.

A more unfortunate first is recorded this year—the first death of an emigrant by an Indian. A man called Pierce was killed on the Truckee River. It should be noted that perhaps part of the blame could be placed on the actions of John Greenwood and Sam Kinney who in 1844 had earlier started trouble with the Indians along the Humboldt. From this year on the Indians, especially the "Diggers" as they were frequently called, became more of a problem, but the major problems facing the emigrants still remained time, distance, food, deserts, and winter.

1845–46 John C. Fremont left on his third official journey of exploration. He explored and traveled through much of the territory along the California Trail, but most of it was not related to the trail and would have little impact on the emigrants' route. He would, however, play a larger role in the California revolt, and this would ultimately impact his career. Walker and Carson acted as his guides during the journey.

1846 This was a major year for both the history of the California Trail and for California because of the revolt and its impact, the continued emigration, and the events surrounding some of the companies.

By December 1845, Fremont was back in California with a larger and stronger military and scientific force than he had had previously in 1844. Having narrowly avoided a conflict with the Mexicans, he left for Oregon. However, in May he was overtaken by a Marine Corps courier, Lieutenant Archibald Gillespie, and after discussions he returned to California in time for the California Revolt. Even today there is still much speculation about what exactly transpired during their meeting and what instructions, if any, Fremont received from Gillespie. Events began to move rapidly, but it must be noted that communications were not as fast as today's. On April 25, Mexican troops had opened fire on General Zachary Taylor's forces at the Rio Grande, and on May 11, President Polk sent a War Message to Congress. Back in California the Americans continued their agitation and William B. Ide, a former school-teacher, proclaimed California an independent republic, the Bear Flag Republic, on June 14, 1846, at Sonoma. Fremont came to the aid of the Americans. Commodore Sloat landed in Monterey on July 7, and the Bear Flag Republic was dissolved and the California fighters joined the US Army as the California Volunteers under Fremont. On July 9, Captain John Montgomery landed in San Francisco and the American flag was raised. While fighting still continued in places the Mexican forces capitulated, and the campaign was over on January 13, 1847, when Fremont and Andies Pico signed an agreement. The formal treaty came in another year.

A large company of Mormons, 238 emigrants, arrived from New York by ship with Sam Brannan as their leader on July 31, 1846. There had been discussions earlier by the Mormons about making California their "Promised Land." However, by the time they arrived Brigham Young had already decided on the Great Salt Lake Valley. Yet, Sam Brannan and these Mormons would still play an important role in the development of California and the California Trail.

Levi Scott and Jesse Applegate opened the Applegate Trail to Oregon. This route was originally blazed eastward beginning in Oregon and meeting the main California Trail along the Humboldt River. Political events, both in Oregon and California, caused many people to think that a southern route to Oregon was needed and that was part of what inspired Scott and Applegate to open their new route. Those wishing to take the Applegate Trail to Oregon left the main Oregon Trail along the Snake River near the Raft River and cut over to the Humboldt leaving it to cross the Black Rock Desert and then entering Oregon from the south. The cutoff from the Humboldt was later incorporated into the Lassen route to California in 1848 and played a major role in the migration of 1849.

While the political status of California was being resolved, another great crisis was developing that has come to be almost synonymous with the California Trail and the hardships faced by the emigrants—the Donner disaster.

The Donner party had been one of the last parties to leave Independence in 1846. Almost from the beginning it seemed to be haunted by delays and problems. At Alcove Spring in Kansas, they experienced their first death, that of Grandmother Keyes. This, however, was not to be their last. Today a marker can be found there, but it is a recent one and a couple of hundred feet from the actual grave site, which is near or directly under the county road by the entrance to the old abandoned parking lot. Here also can be found the stone carved by James Reed with his initials and name. He would play a central role later in the journey. Also carved in the rocks is the name "Alcove Spring," given by Edwin Bryant and carved by George McKinstry, also members traveling together at that time. (See photos of carvings in photo section.)

The Donner party had heard of the Hastings Cutoff and were planning on taking it. However, long before getting to Fort Bridger where they would have to leave the main trail they were warned by James Clyman, a famous mountain man and friend of James Reed, that there was no trail there and that they should not try it, but rather should continue along the established route by way of Fort Hall. However, once at the fort, Jim Bridger seemed to indicate that it was possible. Yet, in reality it had never been tried by wagons. Even the route to Salt Lake had not previously been used as such. Hastings had already started with other wagons to try his new route and was reportedly ready to help guide the Donners if they could catch up. The Donners and some others decided to try it while others in the party decided to follow the established route by way of Fort Hall. Those who took the established route to Fort Hall would reach California without any major problems. The Donners, however, were not able to catch up. They did send

JAMES AND MARGARET REED
Courtesy, California Department of Parks and Recreation

James and Margaret Reed and family are emigrants associated with the Donner disaster of 1846. A few miles east of Pauta Pass near Iron Point, an argument broke out involving Reed. Because of the accidental killing that resulted, James Reed was evicted from the wagon train. His family, however, was allowed to continue with the rest of the wagon company. Although forced to travel on his own, Reed made it safely to California and awaited the arrival of his family. Once word of the fate of the Donner party became known and arrangements could be made for a successful rescue attempt, James Reed led one of the relief parties that helped to bring back his wife, family, and others.

Reed ahead to find Hastings. He did, but Hastings would only "point out" a different and supposedly better route. This new route bypassed the Weber Canyon that the others had taken and crossed the Wasatch Mountains. As the Donners soon found out there was no trail there, and they had to cut their way through. This only delayed them more. Most of this new road would become part of the main route to Salt Lake that the Mormons and others would follow in 1847 and later. Once they got to Salt Lake, they had even more problems. Hastings had reported that the Salt Lake Desert was only about forty miles across, but in reality it was more like eighty miles to Pilot Peak. This was another major error of Hastings.

It now seemed that hardship and delays were constant companions of the Donners. Further down the trail in Nevada, Reed got into a fight with another member and killed him. He was almost executed but was forced out of the company and had to complete the journey on his own while his wife and family remained with the company. Reed finally made it safely to California and was one of the people to lead rescue parties to help the starving and stranded survivors that winter. By the time the Donner party reached the Truckee, winter was fast setting in. As they climbed the mountains they decided to rest. It was a fateful decision because snow fell and blocked the pass. They were forced to remain on the eastern side. They built cabins for protection hoping for a break in the weather which never came. They were soon out of food and none could be hunted. Some tried to get over the mountains on foot, but they were forced back. Starving and desperate with some members already dead and dying, they turned to the only food supply they thought available—the bodies of those members who had already died. The rest is history. There are many books written on the subject for those interested in the complete history and story of their ordeal.

Earlier, while still on the desert, the Donners had sent two members ahead to Sutter's Fort to obtain additional supplies. There they learned that Reed had successfully made it to California, and they related the problems and delays that the Donners had experienced. Later, when the Donners did not show up, Reed and others realized that they were stranded in the mountains, but the California revolt had already started and this delayed rescue missions. By 1847 all those left alive were taken to California. Reed, himself, brought back members of his own family. Out of the Donner party forty members died and forty-seven members survived. It had been the worst disaster on the California Trail. Today names such as Donner Pass, Donner Lake, and Donner Creek all commemorate the tragedy. Hastings was discredited and would never recover his honor and the Hastings Cutoff had seen its day.

1847
This was the year of the major Mormon migration to the Great Salt Lake Valley from the Council Bluffs/Omaha area under the leadership of Brigham Young. The Mormons stayed on the northern side of the Platte River, finally crossing over near Fort Laramie. The route used by the Mormons was later referred to by some as the Mormon Trail, even through much of it coincided with the main Oregon-California Trail. The Mormons opened important ferries to facilitate crossings of the Upper Platte and Green Rivers.

Only about ninety wagons headed for California this year and none tried the Hastings Cutoff.

Charles Hopper led the first company of twenty wagons over the route that cut off from the main Oregon Trail along the Snake River at the raft River. Hopper had been with the Bartleson-Bidwell party in 1841 and Chiles in 1842. Other wagons followed the route cutting off at the Raft River, and this became the main route used from that time on.

1848
This year was a major turning point in the history of California and the California Trail. Many events would occur that would change the course of history, most notably the discovery of gold and the formal takeover of California by the United States.

On January 24, 1848, James Marshall discovered gold in the tailrace in a newly constructed mill on the American River. John Sutter, owner of the mill, wanted to keep it a secret until he could figure out just what to do about it. However, it was a secret that could not be kept. Stories were soon being told and finally on May 8, 1848, Sam Brannan reportedly shouted, "Gold! Gold! Gold on the American River!" on Montgomery Street in San Francisco and word spread like wildfire. Walter Colton Alcalde of Monterey wrote, "The blacksmith dropped his hammer, the carpenter his plane, the mason his trowel, the farmer his sickle, the baker his loafs, and the tapster his bottle. All were off for the mines, some on horses, some on carts, some

JAMES MARSHALL
Courtesy, California State Library

James Marshall was the man who actually discovered the gold that fateful day January 24, 1848 at Sutter's Mill. California was never the same again.

on crutches, and one went in a litter." The gold rush had started!

On February 2 the formal Treaty of Guadalupe Hildago ended the Mexican War. The areas we know of as California, Arizona, New Mexico, Nevada, and Utah were ceded to the United States.

This year also saw many changes in the trail itself. Military forts were being constructed and started to replace the fur company posts. Another route was opened around the Great Salt Lake and two new routes were opened across the Sierra Nevada to California.

The construction of a new fort near Grand Island on the Platte River showed the government's concern about the safety of the emigrants on their westward trek. At first it was called Fort Childs, but it was soon changed to Fort Kearny and replaced the Old Fort Kearny back east on the Missouri. It was built right on the trail and was to protect the emigrants who traveled along the Platte River. Lieutenant Woodbury was in charge of construction, and he had cottonwood trees planted around the parade ground. Today a few of those trees still remain, and as they die they are now being replaced. The fort was finally abandoned in 1871. Today there is a partial reconstruction and a very good museum there.

Captain Samuel Hensley, who had been with Chiles in 1843 was to lead a pack train west to California. He had hoped to head west from Salt Lake City. However, due to terrible hardships on the salt flats, he was forced to return to Salt Lake City. There he decided to follow a new route north toward Fort Hall that had been opened by Hazen Kimball. Hensley decided to follow it north for about eighty miles and then to head west to meet the well-established California Trail. In crossing this section they encountered a creek, which still bears the name given it—Deep Creek. The route joined the main trail near City of Rocks. This route by Hensley cam to be called the Salt Lake Road, the Salt Lake Cutoff, or Deep Creek Cutoff.

A group of Mormons led by Samuel Thompson decided to return to Salt Lake from California. They had been told that the Truckee River route was very hard and too dangerous to travel so they decided to find a new route. They left near present-day Placerville on July 17. Their company included seventeen wagons, forty-five men and one woman. The route they pioneered has come to be called the Carson route. Tragedy Spring was one of their camping grounds where three of their scouts were killed by Indians, and it retains that name today. Further along the route the Hope Valley was also named by them. They picked up a branch of the Carson River and followed it down the eastern side of the Sierra Nevada, and then cut north over to the Truckee route near the Forty-Mile Desert. Then they continued east over the established trail exchanging information about their new trail with westward traveling emigrants. When they came to Steeple Rock (Twin Sisters) near City of Rocks they turned off to follow Hensley's new route—he had met and told them about it—and they arrived in Salt Lake City of September 20.

Joseph Chiles's company of forty-eight wagons was the largest of the California-bound emigrants. It had followed the trail to Fort Hall and then down the Raft and Humboldt. There they also met the Mormons and were told of the new route. When Chiles came to the Humboldt Sink, he turned south along the western side of the Carson Sink and picked up the Carson River, and then followed it until it met the route established by the Mormons. This new sixty-mile section of the Chiles's soon became a major portion of the Carson route. Two other companies led by Clyman and Cornwall also used the new Carson route.

Peter Lassen headed east hoping to bring emigrants back over a route that would end near his ranch. He planned to leave the existing California Trail at what is now Lassen Meadows and then follow the Applegate Trail toward Oregon. He hoped he would find a route that would take him west toward his ranch but he ran into problems. He returned with a wagon company, and they turned off on the Applegate Trial as planned, but he could not discover the route he had hoped to find. He traveled further along the Applegate Trail and finally turned off south near Goose Lake. Within a couple weeks they were in trouble and at one time members of the company even threatened to hand him. Fortunately, two large wagon companies coming from Oregon found the tracks where he turned off the Applegate Trail, and they followed them. One was led by gold hungry Peter Burnett. They caught up with Lassen and with their added strength they were able to cut a new route to Lassen's ranch.

The Lassen Route as it was now called was the third major route to California. However, it was 200 miles longer than the Carson or Truckee routes, given Sacramento as the most common destination. Forty-niners who used this route were misled about claims that it was a short cut.

1849
This was the year of the gold rush and the forty-niner or argonauts. The California Trail was full of people in wagon companies and pack trains. The trail would have to accommodate about fifty times the number of people and animals than it had in the previous year. In this year the make-up of the emigrant also changed. Almost all of the emigrants

were males off to the diggings or for adventure. This was also true for the oceangoing argonauts. It was also the first year for a commercial venture to take emigrants to California. Messrs. Allen and Turner had their Pioneer Line. For two hundred dollars they would take about one hundred twenty people west. Poor planning caused problems and hardship all along the way for them. However, this did not stop commercial ventures, and in following years other tried them.

Joseph Ware's guidebook, *The Emigrants' Guide to California*, was published and became popular with many of the forty-niners. He had never been over the trail but compiled it from reports of others—including Fremont and Sublette. He changed the name of the Greenwood Cutoff to the Sublette Cutoff and also recorded the wrong mileage for the crossing of the desert section of it, making it shorter than it really was. Many an emigrant was very unhappy when they found that out. He made other errors when describing conditions along the Humboldt Valley and sink, calling these areas "rich and beautifully clothed with blue grass." (See a small section of the *Emigrant's Guide to California* in the section on maps and guidebooks.)

On July 19, Benoni M. Hudspeth and John H. Myers broke off from the main trail to Fort Hall just west of Soda Springs near where the Bartleson's party had gone in 1841. But instead of turning south with the Bear River they headed directly west to meet the California Trail later. By doing so they hoped to cut off the loop north to Fort Hall and thereby save both mileage and time. On July 24, they did come to the main California Trail again. Many of the wagons following behind them saw the wagon tracks turn off the main road to Fort Hall and followed them—almost like "the blind leading the blind." Farnham noted on July 20 that the cutoff "now looks like an old road of a great deal of travel." The road to Fort Hall was used less and less by the California emigrants. Yet, J. Goldsborough Bruff, captain of the Washington City and California Mining Association wagon train, followed the Fort Hall road and felt that the cutoff really saved little or no time or mileage.

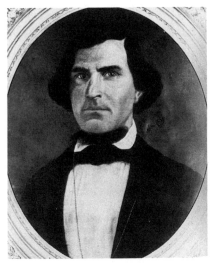

BENONI HUDSPETH
Courtesy, Idaho Historical Society

Benoni Hudspeth's first trip to California was in 1843. In 1849, he served as captain of one of the larger wagon companies headed for California. It was comprised of about seventy wagons and 250 people. They followed the main trail to just west of Soda Springs. Just where the trail turned to the north to Fort Hall, Hudspeth decided to go directly west to meet the California Trail coming down from Fort Hall, thus cutting off miles and saving precious time. Other wagon companies behind Hudspeth followed his wagon tracks and the Hudspeth Cutoff was born. In reality, the twisting cutoff resulted in little saving in time or miles.

The patterns of usage of the various routes shifted in 1849. West of South Pass the route selected by early emigrants was the Salt Lake Road by way of Fort Bridger. Most of the emigrants that came during the middle of the emigration selected the Sublette Cutoff, and those near the end decided to go by way of Fort Bridger. Out in the Great Basin along the Humboldt River a similar pattern developed. The Carson route seemed to be the most popular with the early emigrants while the Truckee route was selected by those during the middle period. Then on August 11 Milton McGee led his wagon company and turned off at Lassen's Meadow and headed up the Applegate or Lassen route. Again those behind started to follow possibly thinking it was the main route. Even Myers and

Hudspeth followed. By the time they discovered what they had done it was too difficult to turn back. On September 19, even Bruff followed. The last emigrants arrived at Lassen's ranch on November 26. Perhaps these shifts were beneficial. If all the emigrants had tried to take the same route the grass and game would have been depleted, and the terrible hardships that did exist would only have been made worse.

1850 Travel along the California Trail doubled that of 1849 with nearly 45,000 emigrants taking the trail. Horses became more popular with the emigrants. Few emigrants would take the Truckee route or the Lassen route, which was now called the "Greenhorn Cutoff." Most emigrants used the Carson route. In this year the emigrants faced even greater hardships than the previous year. Cholera was bad again and took as high a toll as it had in 1849, but the weather conditions were worse and again the increase in usage of the trail took its toll.

California entered the Union as a free state on September 9. Its entrance was made possible by the Compromise of 1850 which balanced the interests of the proslavery groups with those of the antislavery groups. In return for California's entrance as a free state the Fugitive Slave Act was passed, and the Utah and New Mexico territories were organized with the slavery issue to be decided by the residents later.

A trading post sometimes referred to as "Ragtown" was set up on the Carson route after the trail crossed the desert. Further west along the route the Mormon Station was constructed and then in 1851 it was relocated about a mile south of its original location. Both these trading posts had the effect of making the trek easier although prices were certainly not very modest as many an emigrant complained.

All along the trail improvements were being noted by emigrants, and this trend would increase with each year, as new ferries, new bridges, and blacksmith shops sprouted up here and there along the trail. Each year the physical condition of the trail improved.

1851 Fewer people used the California Trail this year but authorities differ on the number. Historian Merrill Mattes, for example, estimates the numbers as high as 5,000-10,000. By now some of the glitter had faded from the gold rush, and emigrants had heard of the terrible hardships along the trail in 1850. Besides, there was Oregon where land was easier to get, and it seemed easier to travel there.

A short but new route was opened at Scotts Bluff through Mitchell Pass. Prior to this the emigrants bypassed the area by going through Robidoux Pass. Today the Oregon Trail Museum is located in Mitchell Pass, and you can walk along the route that was used by so many emigrants and wagons on their way west.

Another branch of the trail was opened by Jim Beckwourth. It turned off the Truckee route north through Beckwourth Pass.

JIM BECKWOURTH
Courtesy, Colorado Historical Society

Jim Beckwourth was the son of a slave and southern planter. He became a mountain man and later guide for the emigrants. He discovered the Beckwourth Pass across the Sierra Nevada.

In September the Treaty of Horse Creek or what has sometimes been called the First Fort Laramie Treaty was signed with the Indians of the Great Plains. The territory was divided into specific tribal grounds, and the US government agreed to provide the Indians with supplies for the next fifty years; the Indians were then to allow the emigrants to pass through their lands unharmed. The peace that this was to ensure did not last very long. Almost immediately some people wanted it changed, and Congress reduced the number of years the Indians were to receive supplies.

1852

This was a banner year for trail travel to California. It was even larger than in 1850. It is estimated that over fifty thousand emigrants including families again traveled over the trails with large herds of cattle and sheep totaling about one hundred thousand. The improvements along the trail were now having their impact. Whereas in 1846 the trip had taken 136 days by ox wagon, this year the fastest made it in 85 days and a mule team did it in 72 days. Unfortunately, cholera was also back on the trail as it had been in 1849 and 1850 and deaths were high.

The Nobles's Road or Nobles' Road was opened. William H. Nobles took the Lassen route to the Black Rock Desert and then headed west across it and along the Smoke Creek Desert. He then crossed the mountains and headed for Shasta City. This was what Lassen had hoped to do earlier. The first wagon company consisted of twenty-six people. This would become a popular route during later years.

Another split in the trail developed on the Carson route. This was called the Johnson's Cutoff. It headed off west to the south shore of Lake Tahoe and then to Placerville. This section replaced part of the section pioneered by the Mormons and became the main route for the next ten years. Today US Highway 50 follows the general route.

The Sonora Road was opened. It was another of the splinter routes that broke off the Carson route. It went south to the

Walker River and then followed it up and over the mountains to Sonora. This was similar to the route taken by the Bartleson Party in 1841. In 1853 this route was heavily used.

Back along the trail just west of South Pass some small cutoffs were also being developed. These cutoffs first followed the trail toward Fort Bridger but turned west near the Green River and later joined the main Sublette Cutoff. They were the Kinney and Slate Creek cutoffs. In a year or so they would be joined by another parallel road the Baker-Davis Road. These became more popular than the main Sublette Cutoff because they cut out the long dry desert crossing of Sublettes Flats.

1853
In 1853 the migration dropped again. However, it was still about twenty thousand emigrants with one hundred fifty thousand head of cattle and sheep.

Another splinter route developed off the Applegate Trail near Clear Lake by the Oregon border. This was the Yreka Road, which took emigrants to northern California and the town of Yreka.

1854
Trouble with Indians increased along the eastern half of the trail in the Platte River Valley. The incident that precipitated the trouble involved a lame cow and an emigrant. The cow wandered off into an Indian village. Instead of trying to obtain the cow back the emigrant continued on to Fort Laramie to get help from the US Army. Lieutenant Grattan, a cannon, and twenty-nine others under his command returned to get the cow. By that time the Indians had already dined on the cow and not much was left. Grattan wanted the Indian responsible for killing the cow. The Indians were willing to give the emigrant a horse in place of the cow, but they were not willing to give up the Indian. Grattan fired the cannon at the village and fighting erupted. When it was over the Brule Chief Bear was dead along with other Indians as well as Lieutenant Grattan and all of his command save one soldier who escaped to tell of the "massacre."

Unfortunately, he died of his wounds two days later. Indians, emigrants, and the army were now at odds and raiding increased for the next couple years.

1855 Travel along the California Trail continued to drop off. This year it was back to the pre-gold rush level and not until 1859 would it almost be back to the 1849 level.

1856 Another splinter developed at the end of the trail. The Big Trees route was opened. It split off the Carson route east of Carson Pass and headed toward Stockton. It was devised by the businessmen of Stockton to divert the emigrant traffic for their own benefit. Improvements were made on the route, and the worst crossings were eliminated by eight bridges with the main bridge being fourteen feet wide and seventy-five feet long. The town even sent out representatives to tell the emigrants of the new road with all its improvements and of all the troubles encountered on the old road.

1857 While the California Trail remained in use traffic was still light. Improvements and additional new routes into California were being developed. Some of them used parts of the California Trail and others bypassed parts of the old routes altogether.

The US Congress appropriated $300,000 for improvements on what was officially referred to as the Fort Kearny, South Pass, Honey Lake Wagon Road, but commonly called the California Trail at least as far as the Lassen Cutoff. Besides improving the grades and crossings, they built reservoirs at places such as Rabbit Hole Spring and Antelope Spring in Nevada, which greatly reduced hardships there.

1858
The Butterfield Stage Line opened. Stage service started at Tipton, Missouri, and then followed the southern route through Texas, New Mexico, Arizona, and then into California.

Fort Bridger was rebuilt by the US Army. It served as a military post until 1890. Nothing was left of Jim Bridger's trading post. Today some of the military buildings have been restored, and it is a living museum and state historic site.

Fort Caspar was established at Louis Guinard's trading post and bridge. It was called the Platte Bridge Station and was named Fort Caspar in 1865 after Lieutenant Caspar Collins who was killed in the vicinity in the line of duty.

Captain Simpson of the topographical engineers developed a new route from the west side of the Salt Lake. It turned south southwest and then almost due west when it crossed the Nevada line to meet the Carson route. Completed in 1859, it soon became popular with the emigrants.

1859
The Lander Road was opened. This was part of the government's improvement plan started in 1857. Frederick Lander started surveying the area near South Pass for a better route. The route he developed cut off east of South Pass near the Burnt Ranch and headed northwest towards Fort Hall thus by-passing the dip to Fort Bridger or the desert crossing of Sublettes Flats. In 1858 work was started on it and it opening in 1859. It soon became widely used by the emigrants of this later period. One estimate for the first year put the emigration at thirteen thousand.

The Central Overland California and Pike's Peak Express was organized. It started at Leavenworth and headed toward Denver and then to Placerville and California. Its route for the most part was different from the established California Trail.

1860s

The Pony Express was established. While it did not last very long it did represent the end of the old era and the beginning of the new. The Pony Express incorporated parts of the California Trail. It started in the east at St. Joseph, Missouri, one of the jumping-off places, and ended at Sacramento, the city that grew up at the site of Sutter's Fort. With the completion of the telegraph in 1861, the Pony Express came to an end.

The 1860s saw more trouble between the settlers and the Indians. Not only did hostilities increase on the California Trail, but also along the Oregon and Santa Fe trails. Fort Churchill was constructed on the Carson route to protect both the emigrants and the growing settlements in the area. Today the area is a Nevada state park.

In one sense, the most significant event of the 1860s which has the greatest impact on the California Trail was the development and completion of the transcontinental railroad in 1869. It often is thought to represent the end of the trail emigration era. In many respects that was true, but for many a poor emigrant the trail west was still the cheapest and only way. The railroad, while not following the complete route, did incorporate parts of the California Trail. Thus, even those who took the "Iron Horse" followed in the footsteps of the early emigrants and argonauts. Today much of Interstate 80 follows the general route of the California-Oregon Trail or one of its branches. ■

Guidebooks

By the end of the 1840s and the early 1850s, the emigrants had a much better idea of where they were going and stood a much better chance of getting there. The earliest emigrants had no guidebooks and knew only vaguely where they were. They largely depended on use of guides or pilots who were usually mountain men, such as Walker, Bridger, Harris, and Greenwood. The knowledge of the area that these men had was important, but so were their skills at survival because often they had to lead emigrants to lands they themselves had never explored. By the mid-1840s, there were enough emigrants themselves who had been over the trails that they began to act as guides or write guidebooks based on their journals. Large sections of the trails were now becoming easier to identify because they had become well-worn. This was especially true of the section where the Oregon and California trails coincided.

Guidebooks went through a type of evolution. The earliest, such as Hastings's, didn't tell much about the specifics of the

Best Guide

to the

GOLD MINES

816 miles

by

IRA J. WILLIS

G. S. L. City

(2)

Thence to the Old Road near .

the Steeple Rocks,   6.

"   to Goose Creek over a hill   10.

192.

Several camping places from the

Steeple Rocks to Goose Creek.

"   up Goose Creek, good camping.   22.

"   to the Hot Spring Valley   13.

"   "   "   2nd Spring   (good camp[)]   5.

"   through the Valley   32.

Found good camping places,

none of them are more than 10 miles apart

"   to a Branch of Mary's River

good camping   8.

"   through a kanyon crossing

the Branch 9 times,   camping   8.

"   to Mary's River   good camping

all along   19.

299.

"   to Martins Fork of Mary's River

good camping all along   60.

· 359·

route but provided more psychological support and encouragement. They soon became more specific concerning the routes and by the time of Ware's guidebooks, frequently included an overall map of the trail. By the early 1850s, the better guidebooks such as Horn's used a milepost approach that had been perfected earlier by Clayton in his guide for the Mormons. Also most of the new guidebooks now included one or more of the new cutoffs that had been developed, such as the Hudspeth, Salt Lake, or Sublette, and bypassed the older main routes by Fort Hall or Fort Bridger.

There were a number of guidebooks that played an important role in the westward movement of the emigrants to California. Some of the better-known ones today are those written by Hastings, Ware, Clayton, Horn, Child, and Marcy. Not so well-known today, but popular among the forty-niners was the small handwritten Willis guide. Portions of some of the above guides will be examined and discussed briefly and the small Willis handbook is included in this volume in its entirety.

Probably the best known early guide is Lansford Hastings's *The Emigrants' Guide to Oregon and California.* It was written in 1844 and printed in 1845. Hastings had gone to Oregon in

Way Bill of distances, camping place, rivers, hot springs etc on the Route from G. S. L. to the Gold Mines — Miles

To Bear River, crossing the Weber 4 miles this side of Capt Brown's Roadometer Measure — 84.
(Good camping at short distances[)]
Thence to Malad or Mud Creek — 3.
" " the 1st Warm Spring — 6.
" " " 2nd do camping — 14.
" " " Spring in the Mts. good camping — 12.
" down deep Creek cross at the Bend — 6.
" " " " good camping — 6.
" to Springs in the plains poor " — 10.
" " Cajiers [or Cajius] Creek good camping at several places in sight on left — 26.
" up Cajiers [or Cajius] Creek, good camping — 9.
176.

(3)
Thence over a hill through a kanyon to where you strike Mary's River again (good camping & good in the kanyon.[)] — 20.
Then to a pass in the hills where you cross the River twice good camping all along — 72.
" " the next crossing of Mary's River good camping all along — 46.
" over a drive without grass or water — 14.
" to the lower crossing of Mary's River (good camping[)] — 14.
" to the lower camping place on the River, grass-scarce — 26.
" to a Slough, poor camping grass scarce — 15.
" " the Sink of Mary's River grass & wood scarce — 20.
The best water here is in a slough that passes through a bend & a narrow Bluff. Here also you may find — 566

1842, moved down to California, and finally returned to the States to encourage more emigrants to go to California. His guide was one of the few available for the earlier emigrants, and it is the one associated with the Donner disaster of 1846. The guide was comprised of fifteen chapters with just over 150 pages. It had, however, only one chapter (nine pages long) devoted to all the routes to California from Canada to the Horn including a proposed new cutoff, which became known as the Hastings Cutoff. (See Jefferson map.) Most of the guide described what was to be found in Oregon and California. One chapter was devoted to preparations and what to bring—this was probably the most useful of all.

The following quotations are from Chapter 14, which was concerned with the different available routes to travel to California and Oregon. First, Hastings described the Oregon Trail west from Fort Hall:

From this fort, those who go to Oregon, continue down Lewis' river, fifteen days, to Fort Wallawalla; and thence down the Columbia, ten days, to the lower settlements in Oregon.

(4)	
a new track on your left that Childs	
intended to make last fall which . _ly be	
nearer & a less distance to do without	
grass & water.	
By the Battalion route from the Sink	
to the hot Springs, no grass, poor water	20.
Thence to Truckie River, good camp.	25.
	622.
	[Should be 631]
The road forks here.	
You will take the left hand road	
to Salmon Trout river good camp	25.
(Childs road if made comes in	
at this or the next camping place[)]	
Then turn to the right and cross a	
bend, good camping	15.
" up the River good camp	8.
" cross a hill to the river good "	12.
" to Pass Creek Kanyon, good	
camping every few miles	42.
" through Pass Creek Kanyon	5.
	738.

(5)	
Then to Red Lake or the foot of the dividing	
Ridge. Calif. Mts	11.
	749.
good camping, nigh by.	
Then to Lake Valley, good camping	6.
" over the highest Ridge to Rock	
Valley, good camping	10.
" to Leek Springs, good camping	
& good by by [*sic*] the way	13.
" " Camp Creek, poor camping	10.
" down the ridge and then you arrive	
into a valley two miles, on your left	
grass plenty	16.
" to Pleasant Valley Go*ld Mines*	12.
	816.
" " Sutters	55.
	861.
	[Should be 871]
Truckie & Salmon Trout are *not*	
the same river but Mary, Ogden &	
Humboldt are.	

From Fort Hall to the Pacific, by the Oregon Route, a distance of about eight hundred miles, there is but one continued succession of high mountains, stupendous cliffs, and deep, frightful caverns, with an occasional limited valley.

This portion of the Oregon route, from Fort Hall to the Pacific, has always been considered, wholly impassable for wagons, or any other vehicles; yet, it is said, that the emigrants of 1843 succeeded in getting their wagons entirely down to the Willamette settlement. This they may have done, but I am confident, from my own experience, that each wagon must have cost the owner of it more time and labor, than five wagons are worth, even in Oregon.

Certainly this was not an encouraging description. Then he described the accepted or old route to California,

Those who go to California, travel from Ft. Hall, west southwest about fifteen days, to the northern pass, in the California mountains; thence, three days, to the Sacramento; and, thence, seven days, down the Sacramento, to the Bay of St. Francisco, in California.

Sounds pretty easy, doesn't it?

Finally he described the geography of both the old and newly proposed routes:

> The California route, from Ft. Hall to the Sacramento river, lies through alternate plains, prairies and valleys, and over hills amid lofty mountains; thence, down the great valley of the Sacramento, to the bay of St. Francisco, a distance from Ft. Hall, of nine hundred miles. The Indians are, in many places, very numerous; yet they are extremely timid, and entirely inoffensive. Wagons can be as readily taken from Ft. Hall to the bay of St. Francisco, as they can, from the States to Ft. Hall; and, in fact, the latter part

LANSFORD HASTINGS
Courtesy, The Bancroft Library

Lansford Hastings was another man who dreamed of creating his own empire. He first traveled west in 1842. Then Oregon was his goal, not California. After a short stay in Oregon, he decided California was the place to make his fortune. However, he is most remembered for his guidebook, the infamous Hastings Cutoff, and its association with the Donner disaster.

of the route, is found much more eligible for a wagon, than the former. The most direct route, for the California emigrants, would be to leave the Oregon route, about two hundred miles east from Ft. Hall; thence bearing west southwest, to Salt Lake; and thence continuing down to the bay of St. Francisco, by the route just described.

It's easy to see how people reading this would head for California. It seemed like only a few easy weeks away by wagon from either Fort Bridger and the new cutoff or from Fort Hall if one took the old route. Hastings even implied that the trip was easier once past the forts. For those emigrants who believed him, they soon learned that he was mistaken. It seemed he was wrong about almost everything from the Indians to the timing and ease of travel over the "lofty mountains." For many of the Donner party they learned too late. Virginia Reed, one of the young survivors, learned her lesson well and put it best, "Never take no cut ofs and hury along as fast as you can."

Joseph Ware's *The Emigrants' Guide to California* was available to the forty-niners and was a fairly popular one, but while better than Hastings's, it was still fairly general for the section of the trail that was exclusively the California section, as can be seen in the following:

> In its course from the Raft river, the road takes a south-western direction, and follows the trail across the dividing ridge to the head of Humboldt or Mary's river, distant one hundred and seventy miles. For two days you travel along the Raft river; camps good. The road over this distance resembles the country west of the South Pass in the Rocky Mountains for the same distance. There are places in which great care is required, and some difficulty may be experienced in consequence of the unevenness of the road in passing over the dividing ridges of the mountains. On the RATTLESNAKE RIVER you can find good camps; there are plenty of good springs also. The prevailing plant is

wild sage, which, in some places, will continue to be your dependence for fuel, though there is some good timber.

We would earnestly advise you to oppose any experiments in your party, in leaving the regular route of travel to try roads said to be shorter. You will get to California in good season if you keep straight ahead. If not, you may lose a month or so of time, and experience the fate of the Donner's party. By trying a new road they lost nearly sixty days, and were overtaken by the snow, and spent the winter in the mountains, where nearly forty of them perished. Lose no time foolishly on the road, that can be spent with profit to yourself and teams. You strike the HUMBOLDT RIVER at its head, from thence your course is down its valley for three hundred miles. It is the principal river of the great basin.

There were two guidebooks authored by Mormons. Ira Willis' [Willes'] *Best Guide to the Gold Mines 816 Miles* was hand-written. He had gone to California with the Mormon Battalion in 1846 and was nearby when gold was discovered at Sutter's, and even worked at the mill. Returning to Salt Lake with the Mormon group that pioneered the Carson route in 1848, they took the new cutoff back to Salt Lake, which had been pioneered by Hensley earlier that year. This route was the one described in his guide. It was the only guide readily available to the forty-niners that really described a solid and traveled route to California. It seems that both James Wilkins and J. Goldsborough Bruff had copies, which they used.

The other Mormon guide was written by William Clayton. His guide was much more specific and accurate, including a milepost approach and detailed information about water crossing, landmarks, obstacles and camping sites. It became the model for later guidebooks of the 1850s. Clayton's guide covered the route to Salt Lake, and Willis' covered it from Salt Lake to California. Compared to Clayton's guide, the Willis version was a Spartan edition, but it was better than anything else and was

Notable Places, Objects, and Remarks.

EAST BRANCH, RAFT RIVER :   12 1171
—25 feet wide; 3 feet deep. The
banks are remarkably soft, and very
bad crossing; a pretty good place to
camp, though but little fuel.

MIDDLE BRANCH, RAFT RIVER :   2 1173
—20 feet wide; 3 feet deep. This, like
the first branch, is very bad crossing,
and about it are many low places, with
good grass.

WEST BRANCH, RAFT RIVER :   5 1178
—25 feet wide; 3 feet deep. A swift
current and gravel bottom, and though
deep, is pretty good crossing; some
willows and grass; here is also the
*junction of the Fort Hall and Califor-
nia roads.*

SWIFT WATER :   5 1183
—12 feet wide. Water and crossing
good, but few inducements for camping; now cross several branches to

FORD NO. 2, W. BRANCH, RAFT RIVER :   3 1186
—2 feet deep. The banks are some-
what soft, but not bad crossing; the
roads are now pretty good to a

Notable Places, Objects, and Remarks.

SMALL BRANCH :   6 1192
—It affords some good water, but cannot be depended on.

ROCK CREEK :   4 1196
—10 feet wide. About one mile before
you reach this you will observe an
old road turning west across the mountain.

SMALL CREEK :   2 1198
—Good water, and early in the season,
good grass.

WHITE CREEK :   2 1200
—20 feet wide. Be cautious about
turning your stock loose here, as there
are several alkali springs to the right
of the road; the old road keeps south
in the valley; the present one passes
over the hills to

CEDAR CREEK :   3 1203
—8 feet wide. Here we find good water, grass, and fuel, and a good place
to camp; you then drive immediately
into

well received. The originals were handwritten and one is
currently in the possession of the National Park Service,
Yosemite National Park, California, who graciously allowed
reproduction from pages of the typeset version.

It seemed that every year new guidebooks were being
prepared and generally they were getting better. A few pages
covering about one hundred sixty miles from *Horn's Overland
Guide* (1852) are included courtesy of the Everett D. Graff
Collection, The Newberry Library, Chicago. Horn's guide included
the Hudspeth Cutoff on the California Trail. In order to compare
it with Hastings' and Ware's, start at "West Branch, Raft River."
This is where the Hudspeth Cutoff joined the main trail coming
down from Fort Hall and the Snake River. Follow it through

Notable Places, Objects, and Remarks.

PYRAMID CIRCLE:*   5   1208
—And pass through it.

JUNCTION GREAT SALT LAKE AND CALI-
FORNIA ROADS: 1   1209
—This is just at the west end of Pyra-
mid Circle, and affords some grass and
fuel, but no water.

SMALL CREEK: 3   1212
—This is the second creek from the
junction; good water, and some fuel
and grass; flat roads.

FLINT SPRINGS AND BRANCH: 4   1216
—In reaching this place you cross a
small creek, about two miles from it;
at this spring and branch you have
good water, and advantages for camping.

* Pyramid Circle is a delightful place. It is 5 miles long, and about
3 miles wide, level within the walls around, and studded throughout
with numerous tall white and green stones, from 60 to 150 feet high,
and 10 to 20 feet in diameter at the foot—some of them running
almost to a point at the top. It is surrounded by mountains which
are covered with pine and cedar trees, and is altogether a beautiful
and picturesque scene. Upon these stones are written, painted, and
engraved, the names of many visitors, with the dates. This circle is
entirely surrounded by the mountains, except an inlet at the east
end of about 50 yards, and an outlet at the west end of about 20
yards.

Notable Places, Objects, and Remarks.

STEEP CREEK: 2   1218
—Just before reaching it you have some
hills and a rough road; down the hill
to the right of the road is some grass
and timber, and a good place to
camp.

OLD ROAD: 3   1221
—Here on a hill an old road leads to
the right; the road is now hilly and
very rough to

BRANCH OF GOOSE CREEK: 1   1222
—10 feet wide. Some grass and fuel,
and good water.

GOOSE CREEK: 3   1225
—25 feet wide; 3 feet deep. The val-
ley of this creek furnishes many good
camping places, and much good grass.

SMALL CREEK: 6   1231
—It is not wide, but very deep, with
soft banks.

RECORD BLUFF, to the left: 10 1241
—It is a sandstone, upon which is writ-
ten the names of thousands of travelers; Good Creek is just to the right;
good camping.

"Pyramid Circle" (City of Rocks) where the Salt Lake Road joined the main California Trail through "Thousand Springs Valley" and finally to the Humboldt or Mary's River. For a comparison, the equivalent section in the Willis guide is from Steeple Rock through Hot Spring Valley to Mary's River. This same section was also covered in the Hastings' and Ware's excerpts, but as can be seen, they were so general that they were of little help for the emigrants. Additionally, both the Willis and the Horn guides used the same general Carson route to cross the Sierra Nevada into California. However, by Horn's time the Carson route had changed some. His guidebook provided added detail, and emigrants felt much more confident with something like this in their hands. ■

Notable Places, Objects, and Remarks.

CAÑON, east end: 4   1245
—The road is quite rough up this *cañon* along a branch of Goose Creek, to a

STONY HILL: 5   1250
—This hill, though rough and rocky, is easily ascended.

THOUSAND SPRINGS VALLEY: 9   1259
—Here we find several small streams of warm water, and some mineral water, but little that is good to use.

SMALL CREEK: 13   1272
—10 feet wide; 2 feet deep. A good place to camp; wild sage for fuel, and tolerable good water, while you find the best of grass.

HOPE SPRINGS: 24   1296
—You will find considerable branch water all along before you come to this spring, but it contains the very best of water; you will now go south to the mouth of a

CAÑON: 1   1297
—Where you will find some grass, and a good place to camp.

Notable Places, Objects, and Remarks.

CAÑON CREEK: 9   1306
—6 feet wide. Good water, but no grass; you will pass over a rough road for some distance to

DECEPTION VALLEY: 18   1324
—This valley from the surrounding hills has the appearance of a beautiful meadow, but it is all weeds.

DEEP FORK (of Humboldt):   5   1329
—12 feet wide; 4 feet deep. The water is clear, and current swift; some grass and fuel, and a fair place to camp.

HUMBOLDT RIVER: 6   1335
—3 rods wide; 5 feet deep. It is very bad crossing, and within one mile you cross two other branches of it, which are also bad; the roads are then good down the river to

WEST BRANCH, HUMBOLDT RIVER: 23   1358
—4 rods wide; 4 feet deep. A solid gravel bottom, and good crossing; no grass.

Diaries

Emigrant diaries came in all sizes and shapes. Each emigrant had their own style. Some like Bruff's (1849) were extremely detailed and illustrated. Others like William Baker's (1852) had only a line or two for each day. Some wrote regularly and others infrequently. Merrill Mattes, eminent historian and authority, suggests that about one out of 250 emigrants kept some form of written record of their journey.

For the historians these diaries are the major source of insights into the trail's history and the emigrants themselves. Yet, no single diary can be considered the definitive one. Conditions on the trail could change in a few days, let alone from one year to the next. Different portions of the trail had different characteristics and demands. The organization, planning, and leadership of the wagon company varied but was crucial. Even the character of the particular emigrant had its impact. Each wrote from his/her own perspective, interest, and expectations. Men and women saw things differently. All these factors combined to give each emigrant their own special reaction to the trail and, thus, was reflected in their diary and made it different from other diaries.

Well-run companies and poorly-run ones shared the trail at the same time and place. Some companies ran out of supplies early, while others still had some to discard or to share with those less fortunate. For some companies it seemed that things were always going wrong, while others had no serious problems. Therefore, one diarist would report a very different impression of the trek west from another. This is not meant to say that they did not have similar experiences, however. Only by examining a variety of diaries can one fully understand the trek west.

The following diary excerpts are from those of three emigrants: James Wilkins (1849), The Henry E. Huntington Library and Art Gallery; Wakeman Bryarly (1849), Yale University Library; and Eleazar Ingalls (1850), The Newberry Library. The diaries are "typical" in that length, varied greatly and the three excerpts give insight into what it was like on one major section of the trail. The impact of the different factors and conditions that combined to give them their own personal experience come through clearly to the reader.

By the time the emigrants had reached the Mary's or Humboldt River they had come about sixteen hundred miles, depending on where they began. Yet the worst part of the California Trail still faced them—crossing of the great desert area and then the climb over the Sierra Nevada. If the emigrants hadn't seen it already, this is where they got a close look at the "elephant," the symbol of hardships and despair. Come join our three diarists as they leave the Humboldt Sink and head off to cross the Forty-Mile Desert area for either the Truckee (Salmon Trout) River or the Carson River and climb the Sierra Nevada. Emigrants traveling on the Lassen Route had already turned off at the Meadows and had had to contend with the Black Rock Desert. Their experiences were similar to those that will be noted in the following passages. Bryarly would head west for the Truckee, while Ingalls and Wilkins would cut southwest to the Carson.

Notice their comments concerning earlier expectations, the problems of their own wagon company and others, the climatic and physical conditions found and endured on the desert, and its general impact on their own feelings and future expectations. Remember also, the account of Betsey and Ike in the song at the beginning.

Read along and relive their journey as they headed west through the deserts and over the mountains.

— □ —

Wakeman Bryarly, 1849

Bryarly left St. Joseph, Missouri, on May 10, 1849, and took the Sublette Cutoff. He then went by way of Fort Hall because the Hudspeth Cutoff was not opened when he passed. He reached the sink on August 11 and the Truckee on the thirteenth. The ascent up the Truckee took the emigrants to Donner Lake. On August 22, Bryarly made the final ascent up Roller Pass, not Donner Pass. On September 11, 1849, he arrived at Johnson's ranch.

Since Saturday at 2 o'clock, we traveled 65 miles without *wood* or *water* to last evening (Monday) at 6 o'clock.

Saturday, August 11th.

The morning was fair, beautiful, & pleasant. Early, everything & everybody was in active preparation for a start in the evening. Grass was bundled & packed & stowed in the wagons. Loose mules were packed also, & everyone riding an animal had his fodder behind him. Casks & kegs, gum bags & gun covers, coffee pots & tea kettles, canteens, jugs & bottles, *everything* was filled with water & at 1 o'clock the order to gear up was given & at 2 we bid farewell to the marsh & our numerous friends. The road goes direct across to strike the old road some 5 miles . It was a new one, & made through the sage bushes & of course was not very good, but the old road was as smooth as a table & hard as a rock. It passed over what is in high water part of the sink & consequently there was no vegetation save a few sage bushes, which were upon mounds several feet above the level. Stock of all sorts, horses, mules, oxen & cowss were scattered along, having corralled themselves in the arms of fatigue & death. Here for the second time upon our journey we saw the mirage upon these immense white basins. It was a poor example, however, but was very deceiving to those who had never seen anything of the kind before.

Twelve miles upon the old road brought us to the *Sink*, the desideratum of long hoped for weeks. "How far to the Sink?" has been a question *often* asked & *often* answered, & *often* heard in the last month. This Sink extends over several miles & is generally grown up with rushes & grass. There is immense basins however on all sides, which, in high water, receive the back water. The road keeps in these basins, which extend over *miles & miles* without a vestige of vegetation, but so white & dazzling in the sun as scarcely to be looked at. We rolled by this, the water of which cannot be used by man or beast, (for) 4 miles, & came to some sulphur springs or rather wells. Here we encamped for the night. These wells were dug in a slough, & the water was very like many of our sulphur springs at home. The animals drank it freely & it seemed to do them no harm. In this slough just below the spring were a great number of cattle & mules, which had become mired & were not able to get out & were left. Some of them were still alive. The most obnoxious, hideous gases perfumed our camp all night, arising from the many dead animals around. In the morning some were found laying immediately by us & in the vicinity 30 others were adding their scents to the nauseous atmosphere. Our animals were turned to the grass we brought already dried, & they seemed (to) relish it much.

We were *past the Sink*. I would ask the learned & descriptive Mr. Fremont & the elegant & imaginative Mr. Bryant, where was the beautiful valley, the surpassing lovely valley of Humbolt? Where was the country presenting the most splendid "agricultural features?" Where the splendid grazing, the cottonwood lining the banks of their *beautiful meandering stream*, & everything presenting the most interesting & picturesque appearance of any place they ever saw?

Perhaps Mr. Bryant was speaking ironically of all these most captivating things that he saw, or perhaps he thought it was "too far out" for anyone else but himself to see. If not, I have only to say, "Oh shame where is thy blush."

We have travelled along it several hundred miles, from its commencement from a little pool that you could drink up if thirsty, to its termination in the sink. It is so very crooked in its whole course that I believe it impossible for one to make a *chalk mark* as much so. Frequently I have stood & fished on each side of me in two different parts of the river, the distance around being half a mile or more. It is a *dirty, muddy, sluggish, indolent stream,* with but little grass at the best of times, & as for cottonwood, there is not a switch of it from one end to the other. A friend of mine remarked, it was fit for nothing else but to sink to the "lower Regions," & the quicker it done it the better. He much preferred calling it Hellboldt River.

Distance, 23 miles.

Sunday, August 12th.

We rolled out at daybreak. The road was firm, hard, level, & smooth. In four miles we came to the forks of the road. Here we found many placards, the most of which advised their friends to take the right. The left was but little travelled in comparison to the right, & we took it. We rolled through the same kind of a basin as yesterday and at 10 miles we stopped to breakfast, which was cooked with some pieces of wagons we picked up on the road. We layed by until 2 o'clock having given grass & water to our stock, & again rolled. The road continued the same for several miles, when we left the basin forever, the road then being upon a ridge with a few sage bushes & rocks. We rolled thus 15 miles, which brought us to the Hot Springs.

Seventy dead animals were counted in the last 25 miles. Pieces of wagons also, the irons in particular—the wood part having been burnt—were also strewn along. An ox-yoke, a wheel & a dead ox; a dead ox, yoke, & wheel; & a wheel, dead ox & a yoke, was the order of the day, every hundred or two yards.

These Hot Springs are one of The things upon this earth. The pool is some 25 or 30 yds. in circumference & around it are a great number of springs, some placid & luke warm, others sending off considerable steam & hot water, & others again, bubbling & boiling furiously & scalding. The water when cooled was drinkable, but sulphurish & very salt. There was a great number of kegs & casks, boxes & wagonbeds here, which had been used to cool the water by others. These we filled & after some hours our stock drank it. A piece of meat, held in one (of) the boiling springs, boiled in 20 minutes, perfectly done. By putting the water in your coffee-pot & holding the pot over the bubbling, it would boil in a few minutes. In this way many of us cooked our suppers.

Thousands of dollars worth of property thrown away by the emigration was laying here. Wagons & property of every kind & description, not saying anything of dead animals & those left to die. The machinery of a turning machine that must have cost $6(00)or $700. A steam engine & machinery for coining that could not have cost less than $2(000) or $3000, were also laying here, all sacrificed upon this Jornado. These things they say belonged to the notorious Mr. Finley (?) who also lost 55 cattle out of 80.

Distance, 25 miles.

Monday, August 13th.

We started this morning (at) 2 1/2 o'clock. The road was again in a basin & was level, hard, & smooth. Soon after daylight our animals showed evident signs of fagging. Four miles from the Hot Spring we came to some sulphur springs. They were very salty & not good, but had been used by others. The sun was most powerful, & the reflection from the shining dirt made it most oppressive. We rolled 12 miles, & having come to where we strike the sand which we have been dreading all the time, we stopped to breakfast. some of our teams did not get in for some time after the others, they having fagged so much as to fall in the rear.

Here we fed the last of our grass & gave the last of our water. Several wagons were here, the animals having given out & were taken to the river ahead to recruit, which we learned was but 8 miles, but deep sand all the way. Several of us started soon after eating & came on to the river & luxuriated ourselves & horses with delicious water. The teams started at 1 o'clock but finding they would in all probability give out or at least be a dead strain all the way, they determined to double teams & bring half over & recruit the mules & bring the remainder today. This was accordingly done & seven wagons arrived safe & our animals watered & turned to good grass. Some remained behind with the wagons & water was packed back to them.

This (is) Salmon Trout (Truckee) River. It is a beautiful clear, swift stream, & the water is delicious. Large cottonwood trees skirt its banks, which gives everything around an air of comfort once more. In approaching it the trees are seen a mile off, & to the parched, famished, & wearied man & beast they are truly "a green spot in the desert." We are safely over *the desert,* however, without losing a single animal, although many are very far gone; but a day or two recruiting, which we think of giving them here, will put them again all right. The water of the Hot Spring which was used freely by both the men & animals affected them most singularly. Two or three hours after drinking, it produced violent strangling to both. The men in particular were very much annoyed also by the most violent pain in the urinary organs. It was truly laughable to see their contortions & twistings after urinating, which they desired to do every hour. The mules also seemed to suffer much, but their symptoms lasted only 10 or 12 hours. Upon examining an old canteen that had had this water in it, with a grass stopper, I discovered the evident fumes of nitre, & upon examination found it (to) contain much, & no doubt these unpleasant symptoms were caused by it. The dead animals were not so numerous today although there was yet sufficient to be very annoying from their perfumes. On the other (Carson) road I am told they are much thicker, more than half of the head emigration having taken that road.

Distance, 20 miles.

Tuesday, August 14th.

All night the teams, with loose mules & oxen, were rolling in, causing a general buzz all night. We layed in camp until noon, our mules being in excellent grass. They were then brought up & taken back (on the desert) for our remaining teams, which arrived in camp at 12 o'clock at night. They report many more dead animals upon the road than yesterday. Every train that has arrived has lost one or two upon this last stretch. The weather today was most oppressively hot & we congratulated ourselves we were not on the parched desert.

There is two roads here, one to the left on the same side of the river with a stretch through the sand of 25 miles to water & grass, the other crosses the river & keeps up the river through a kanyon 16 miles & crossing the river many times. From all we have been able to gather, we have determined to cross the river, taking the right hand road. We had today a general inspection of our provisions & find we have only sufficient to last us ten days. This was alarming & our Quartermaster was ordered to look out for more.

Wednesday, August 15th.

All night the starved & famished mules & cattle were rushing through our camp, very much to the annoyance & risk of injury to those sleeping upon the ground. Many teams arrived last night, with the same proportionate loss as those before them. Everyone, without a dissenting voice, cursed the desert, and yet thank God they are over it with their little loss.

The morning was again very hot & we almost dreaded the idea of exposing ourselves to the hot rays of the sun upon the road. Our mules were brought up at 11 o'clock & we again hooked up. We crossed the river & rolled two miles when we came to a sand bluff which was very hard pulling. We passed upon this one mile & a half & nooned, turning our mules across the river to grass, it being the only grass in several miles. Our Quartermaster having made arrangements to obtain some flour & pork from a train behind, the sick wagon was left to bring it when it should arrive. One mile from noon we got off the sand & crossed the river & was soon in the kanyon proper. We passed along this, crossing the river four times in 5 miles. Here night overtook us, & not being able (to) proceed farther, & finding Capt. Smith awaiting us, we pulled out on the side of the road & tied our mules to the wheels, feeding them upon willows & cotton bushes.

Owing to the scarcity of the grass, the Captain determined to keep a camp ahead (of us), & leave (some) one behind at each place to point out the grazing spots, & I (am) to remain behind to take charge of the train. Our herders have been reduced to the ranks, each teamster taking care of his own extra mules, & the other extra ones rode by the men.

A fellow statesman & friend, Mr. Long, having overtaken us today, invited Mr. Washington to accompany him through (to the diggings), he being upon pack mules & expecting to arrive a week before us. I tendered to him (Mr. Washington) the use of my "Walking Squaw" & he determined to accept & started off an hour before us. By the way, the Hot Spring water acted very singularly upon the "Squaw." Soon after arriving at breakfasting on the morning of the 13th at the beginning of the sand, she was taken with violent pain, as though she had the cholic, & very much to the astonishment of all, she was *confined* & brought forth. This abortion no doubt was caused by the water. We know not her history &

consequently cannot tell the pedigree of the little one, or whether she herself had been *imprudent & slipt her foot,* but who knows but in this, was lost the race of as fine stock as ever the world saw. "Squaw," with her nation's peculiarity, was as much herself again in half an hour as though nothing had happened, & was hitched to the sick wagon & dragged it through the sand to the river. (The power of endurance of some of these ponies is most astonishing.)

Distance, 8 miles.

Thursday, August 16th.

We had a most unpleasant camp last night, & at daylight we were again upon the road. Yesterday evening it clouded up with heavy black clouds, with rolling, rumbling thunder, accompanied with vivid flashes of lightening. In the course of half an hour we were blessed with a hail storm, with a fine shower of rain. This is the first for 7 weeks & we hailed it with delight. Last night it was cloudy & very dark, with distant thunder, & being (in) the very narrow place in which we were, with high mountains upon each side, and only able to see the sky looking straight up, gave it a most dismal and sepulchral appearance, & daylight was most welcomed. We rolled 3 miles & coming to some grass upon a flat we stopped to breakfast. Here we remained 2 hours & again rolled 5 miles, when we came to better grass & corralled for the day for the purpose of waiting for our provision train, as well as to feed our mules.

We crossed the river today 7 times, making 12 times in all. Some of them were deep & very rocky, with a swift current, so much so as to take some of our mules off their feet. It was amusing to see many of our men riding their mules across. They would do it most cautiously, picking out their way in every step, but in spite of all this, they would frequently fall, sometimes rolling over (on) their sides & corralling them the riders most beautifully in the water. Our friend Locke, in particular, was riding "a very high mule" whose legs were "twisted out"—& which landed him most beautifully in Salmon Trout. The current is so strong that a man can but with difficulty walk across, & consequently it is very dangerous to be thrown in. As yet everything has passed in safety & we hope, with care, it will continue to be so.

Distance, 8 miles.

Friday, August 17th.

It rained again last night & a very heavy dew also fell. We started at 6 o'clock & crossed, & recrossed the stream. Eight miles we nooned, crossing in this distance 8 times. Here we had tolerable grass, our Captain having picket it, & left one (of the advance) to point it out to me. We remained here until 2 when we again rolled. In the evening, we rolled 7 miles, crossing the river 4 times, making in all 22. (24.)

The road between the crossings was sandy in some places, rocky in others, & very steep both going up & coming down in others. After 7 miles we emerged in a beautiful, green, velvety valley, which, upon first coming in view, presented a most cheering appearance. We here crossed a slough, the crossing of which was fixed & bridged by our Captain & party ahead. Before this was done, it is said it was almost impassible, each having to be cordelled across. We passed over in safety & encamped in this lovely valley, with blue grass to the horses' knees. We passed today two graves; one had been drowned several days before, the other had died today. We came in sight for the first time of the Sierra Nevada mountains, or rather of the chain. During the day it has been cloudy, with constant rumbling of thunder in the distance. In the morning we had a very nice shower, & several times during the day it gave us a pleasant sprinkle.

Distance, 15 miles.

Saturday, August 18th.

It was our determination to lay here until the provision train should arrive, consequently we endulged in an uncommon knap after sunrise. Grass was fine, wood plenty, & water delicious, with a beautiful cam, & we all enjoyed it very much. Grass was mowed & packed, & in the evening we hooked up & moved up the valley 3 miles so as to be nearer the stretch of 15 miles for which we prepared the grass. Two men were left here to conduct the (provision) wagon over the slough & bring them up to us.

Distance, 3 miles.

Sunday, August 19th.

The provisions did not arrive last night, very much to our disappointment, but today about 9 o'clock it came in sight, when immediately we hooked up & rolled out. We soon left the valley, the road being very rocky with large round stones. In six miles we struck the river, where we nooned, giving some of our grass to them the animals.

Upon a proposition, the flour & bacon was divided between the different messes, on account of the scarcity of the provisions & thinking that they would be more economical in using them.

We rolled out at 2 o'clock. The road was rough in the extreme & very hilly. We crossed the river 4 times making 26 (28) times altogether. Ten miles we came to the river again. Before striking it we came to large trees of pine, cypress, & lignum vitae. The banks of the river & the sides of the mountain are also covered with them. The valley where we strike the river is narrow, but had excellent grass upon it, but by some person or persons unknown, (it) was burned off & part of it was still burning. We tied up to the wheels & fed the remainder of the grass we had provided ourselves with yesterday.

Distance, 16 miles.

Monday, August 20th.

The scenery around us last night would put at defiance the artist's pencil. It was one of the most majestic ones that ever falls to the lot of man to witness. Immediately upon the opposite side of the river, the mountain commenced its ascent, covered with large timber of fur, pines of all sorts, & arbor vitae. They were not thick but presented rather, the appearance of a grove with good verdure & no underwood. The valley was narrow but was visible for a mile or more. In a thousand different places, both on the side of the mountain and along the valley, the trees & grass had been set on fire. It was a dark night, the clouds having gathered over very threateningly at sundown, & the bright blazing fires up the mountain and down the valley, the roaring & splashing of the river over the rocks, accompanied with the occasional fall of a tree that had burned through, with the howling of wolves *(one word illegible)* in their round, all presented a scene to the wearied & silent beholder not soon to be forgotten.

We started at daybreak & crossed the river. The road turned immediately to the right in a north direction & continued for one mile, when it went in a northwest direction, ascending a spur of mountain, one of the chain of the California mountains. We ascended this, it being in some places very steep, & then again coming upon a little table of land upon which had been good grass, & upon one with a cool but small spring. After rolling there 5 miles, we opened upon a beautiful little valley with a very steep hill to descend to it. We went down in the valley & nooned. This valley is oval in shape & had plenty of good grass & water in it.

We rolled again at 2 P.M. The road here took a south direction, having travelled northwest this morning. We passed along through the woods, which was very large timber of the same description as before described. Occasionally we struck a little valley with good grazing & water. Four miles we encamped in one of these valleys. At our noon today we learned from a gentleman, that the Indians had killed one of his mules with an arrow last night. They were about starting in search of them.

Distance, 9 miles.

Tuesday, August 21st.

It was very cold last night & many of us that had not prepared for it suffered much from it. The grass was covered with a white hoary frost, which crackled under our feet. The water in our buckets was frozen to considerable thickness. We started early & rolled over the same kind of road as yesterday evening, through woods, valleys, & up & down hill, but none very steep. Three miles brought us to a larger valley than usual, with a little stream of water coming from the mountains on our right. This is one of the tributaries of Truckee or Salmon Trout. We rolled 6 miles over the same sort of country with high mountains upon each side of us & came to another large valley with a larger stream running through it—another tributary to Salmon Trout. Here we nooned.

Around our camp last night the awful & distressing cries of a panther was heard, first in one place, then soon after in another. The guard came in one after another to double arm themselves for this very formidable enemy, but he did not return too near. Today, one was seen only a short distance from camp, in the road. He stopped & turned to take a survey of those behind, & then trotted slowly away. They had no rifle & consequently did not pursue.

We rolled in the evening at 2 P.M. The road still the same, except a little rougher. Four miles, the road turned left. Here, upon our left, distant some hundred yards from the road was Truckee River in all its glory again, splashing & dashing over the rocks. Here we met one of our advance who informed us we were but five miles from the base of the *great bugaboo,* that which has caused many a sleepless night, with disturbed dreams to the discouraged emigrant, *"The Sierra Nevada" Mountains.* We were much inspired & equally rejoiced, as we had no idea we were so far on our way. We were informed there was no grass at the base, or near it, & consequently we rolled a mile or so farther & encamped.

We were informed that the cabins of the "Lamentable Donner Party" were also on our road, as well as also (that) the (Pyramid, or Donner) Lake (was) but one mile from the present trail. I immediately started off to look for these mournful monuments of human suffering. One was only 150 yds. from our camp upon the left of the trail. This (cabin) was still standing. It was two in one, there being a separation of logs between. The timbers were from 8 inches to a foot in diameter, about 8 or 9 ft. high & covered over with logs upon which had been placed branches & limbs of trees, dirt &c. The logs were fitted very nicely together, there being scarcely a crevice between. There was one door to each, entering from the north and from the road.

There were piles of bones around but mostly of cattle, although I did find some half dozen human ones of different parts. Just to the left of these was a few old black burnt logs, which evidently had been one of those (cabins) which had been burnt. Here was nearly the whole of a skeleton. Several small stockings were found which still contained the bones of the leg & foot. Remnants of old clothes, with pieces of boxes, stockings, & bones in particular, was all that was left to mark that it had once been inhabited.

In the centre of each was a hole dug which had either served as a fireplace or to bury their dead. The trees around were cut off 10 ft. from the ground, showing the immense depth the snow must have been. After examining this I passed on one mile where the road went to the left in a more southerly direction. The old trail went on straight down the valley to the Lake which was distant one mile. I went on to the lake & was fully repaid for my trouble, for it was one of the most beautiful ones on record. It was beautiful, fresh, pure, clear water, with a gravelly bottom, with a sandy beach. It was about 2 miles long, three-quarters wide & confined between three mountains on three sides, which arose immediately from its edge.

On the other (side) was the valley by which I had approached it & through which a little stream was passing off from it. I here took a delightful bath & felt renovated.

In returning I came to another of the cabins, but which had been burned by order of Gen'l Kearney. Here also I found many human bones. The skulls had been sawed open for the purpose, no doubt, of getting out the brains, & the bones had all been sawed open & broken to obtain the last particle of nutriment.

Bryant has given a most satisfactory account of the suffering of the unfortunate emigrants of Donner's party & the many trials, deprivations & sufferings, with loss of life (that) runneth not in the knowledge of man. To look upon these sad monuments harrows up every sympathy of the heart & soul, & you almost hold your breath to listen for some mournful sound from these blackened, dismal, funeral piles, telling you of their many sufferings & calling upon you for bread, bread.

There seems to be a sad, melancholy stillness hanging around these places, which serves to make a gloom around you, which draws you closer & closer in your sympathies with those whom hunger compelled to eat their own children, & finally to be eaten by others themselves, & their bones now kicked perhaps under any one's feet. There was also another cabin upon the opposite side of the road, but I did not visit it.

Accompanying the Pittsburgh (Company) was a man by the name of Graves, who was one of the survivors of this party. I conversed with him several times about the road when meeting with him upon (the) trip, but he avoided & alluded (i.e. eluded) any conversation about his misfortune. I was told by a member of his Company, that the night before they came to this place, Graves started off without saying anything to them, & did not (re)join them until after they had passed. He preferred viewing the place of his unprecedented suffering alone, not wishing that the eye of unsympathising man should be a witness to his harrowed feelings.

A meeting of our company was called today & our Quarter-Master was appointed to select two other gentlemen to go ahead of us, to obtain provisions necessary for us upon our arrival, & also to find out all the important information necessary for us to commence operation in the mines. They accordingly, this afternoon, left us, having their provender tied on behind them.

Distance, 14 miles.

Wednesday, August 22nd.

It was very cold again last night, & it occurred to us forcibly that if it was this cold here in August, what must it be in January. Early everything was in motion. In one mile we crossed a little stream to the left, which runs from the Lake. Here we stopped, & cut sufficient grass for a feed. After rolling one mile farther we struck the foot of the mountain. The Road was very rough & in many places steep both going up & coming down. Every n ow & then there was a little table upon which was a little grass. We rolled thus 2 miles when we nooned (or rather rested, not taking our mules out) upon one of these tables. We stopped 2 hours, when we ascended a steep & very rocky road with many short turns around the large rocks & trees. One mile brought us to the foot of the "Elephant" itself. Here we "faced the music" & no mistake. The "Wohaughs" could be heard for miles, hollowing & bawling at their poor cattle who could scarcely drag themselves up the steep acclivity.

We immediately doubled teams, & after considerable screaming & whipping, thus arrived safe at the top. They then returned & took up the remainder with like success. We were but four hours ascending, & we were much disappointed, but agreably so, in not finding it much worse. Certainly this must be a great improvement upon the old road, where the wagons had to be taken to pieces & packed across. We rolled down the mountain 4 miles, the road being rough & steep half way & then striking a valley, where it was good. We passed through a grove of woods & then emerged into a beautiful valley & encamped.

We were all in the most joyous & elated spirits this evening. We have crossed the only part of road that we feared, & that without any breakage, loss or detention. I had but the one & only bottle of "cognac" that was in our camp, & which I had managed to keep since leaving the Old Dominion. This I invited my mess to join me in, & which invitation was most cordially accepted. When lo & behold, upon bringing it out, it was empty—yes positively empty. The cork was bad & with numerous joltings, it had gradually disappeared. This was a disappointment many of us will not soon forget.

Distance, 8 1/2 miles.

--------------------------------- □ ---------------------------------

James Wilkins, 1849

Wilkins left Weston on May 8, 1849. On September 9, he arrived at the sink, and the Carson River by September 10. The next two weeks were spent recruiting, ie., resting their stock and themselves, and then continuing up the Carson River. On September 23 the climb up the mountains commenced, and on October 16, 1849 Wilkins arrived at Sutter's Fort.

Sunday Sepr 9th

Came only about 18 miles since our last encampment to this place, where we have been laying two days, cutting hay. we are now about 15 miles from the sink, and as we have found unexpectedly good grass, we think it better to lay in our supply here for the desert, and recruit our cattle, than to risk going further, for all is uncertainty and rumour about the road in advance. This is the last good water we shall have for 70 miles they say, and we are filling every vessel that will hold it. The great object of dispute amongst us now is which of the two roads we shall take, that we are informed branch off from the sink over the desert. The old road or what is called Child's road. the reports about them are so contradictory, that we do not know what to do. Provissions are getting very scarce along the road among the emigrants generally. we have as much hard bread and bacon left as is necessary, but our sugar flour vinigar beans dried apples in fact everything else is gone, and we must see hard times before we reach California. The last barren country we have passed thro' has told hard upon our cattle—and others too, if we may judge by the number of dead cattle we passed the last 18 miles. We expect to leave here some time to night, and go down to the sink by daybreak so avoid the midday sun, as the reflection from it on the sand makes it intensely hot in the middle of the day, and distresses our cattle very much. Scurvey is becoming very prevalent among the emigrants. we have heard of several deaths with it—

(This entry opened with five and a half lines which Wilkins later struck out: "I wish California had sunk into the ocean before I had ever heard of it. here I am along, having crossed the desert it is true, and got to some good water. but have had nothing to eat all day, my companions scattered, our wagons left behind. that desert has played h—l with us.")

Wednesday 12th

We arrived at the sink late in the night [Sunday, September 9], having it 25 miles instead of 15, the water poisonous, and not a spear of grass. we pushed on near 3 miles further to where some holes had been dug in the ground, and water strongly impregnated with sulphur had been found. but few of our cattle would touch it, thirsty as they must have been. here we rested 2 or 3 hours till the moon rose, gave them some hay and pushed on into the desert, 45 miles to the next water. we took the left hand road or Childs cut off, as it is called and travled till eleven the next day [September 10], when we stopped and fed the oxen and ourselves. Wide plains of sand salt lying thick on the ground in some places, with here and there a few bushes of greasee wood. the mirage exists here. lakes of water, appearently but a few miles from us. About one O'clock, the D--- and I rode off to go thro' leaving the wagons to follow. here commenced the great distruction of property. abandoned waggons dead catle and articles of every discription lay strewed along the road. between that time and dark, that is for the next 16 miles I counted 163 head of dead stock oxen mules and horses, 65 wagons, some of them entire, others more or less demolished, about 70 ox chains, yokes, harness, trunks, axes, and all minor things I did not count, and these only while riding along the road. doubltess there were a great many I did not see. holes had been dug in different places for water, but it was so strongly impregnated with salt, as to be scarcely drinkable. about dusk we came up with the pioneer wagons left on the road, their mules being unable to drag them further. they had taken them out and drove them on to the river to recruit. the passengers those that were able walked on. but there were a great many sick, and unable to walk. these had to stay with nothing but salt water to drink. amongst them a Mr James was expected to die with scurvey. they like us had nothing left but bread and bacon, and for these they were indebted to the ox teams on the road. three dollars a pint was offered for vinegar. A soft heavy deep sand commenced here, and continued to the river, (about 10 miles,) thro which our horses laboured severely. we sighed for our cattle, and judging from the smell which saluted our nostrils every few minutes, for it was dark they must have lain pretty thick on the ground. here we met Turner going back with a few mules to fetch one of this wagons containing those most severely sick. About 10

O'clock we arrived at the river and found the pioneer passengers asleep around an immense log fire, for here are actually some large cotton wood trees, the first we had seen since leaving the settlements. We toasted a slice of bacon and eat a cracker that we had brought with us, and lay down beside the fire to sleep. I did not res much it being too cold, but got up and sat by the fire till morng. At day break [September 11] the Dr returned to meet the wagons, which he met about 6 miles back found several of the oxen had given out, so he concluded to leave them for the day and drive on the oxen to water and grass to recruit.

Thursday 13th

All day yesterday I was alone huntg our boys, without successs till evening. I met E P--- he informed me of the condition of things. several of the oxen still back in the desert. I lent him my mule to ride back and fetch them in, and to bring some bed clothes and provissions, and to meet me at the Pioneer herdsmens camp two miles down the river, where they had driven the rest of the cattle for grass, there being none nearer. Thither I went and waited all night but he came not. this morng early I set off, determined to find some one that would give me a breakfast. I met E P--- coming on my mule. it seems they were unable to get the cattle down last night but gave them some hay they had, and stayed at the upper camp, or where the road first strikes the river, where he told me to go, and I should find some provissions. I accordingly came on, and got some hot wter slightly colored with coffee, and hard bread. to night we shall get up the oxen and fetch in the wagons if we can.

Sunday 16th

We only left our campg ground near the Pioneer's last evening, having been detained by fetching in from the desert 6 or 7 miles back an abandonned wagon, which it was said was much lighter than one of ours, and a good wagon. but after it was brought in and examined by the parties interested, it was risolved to take the old one so by shortening her up and cutting two feet off the bed, and otherwise lightening her, it was thought the teem would pull her thro'. All our cattle are much exhasted and reduced in flesh, as well as other peoples'. I pity those families very much and tremble for their safety that are a week or two behind. Mr James of the pioneers died and was buried yesterday, "with a blanket wrapt around him." what a tale of suffering and neglect he could tell, if the dead could speak. Turner offers 500$ to any one that will fetch in his provission wagons 3 in number and about 16 miles out, but no emigrants have teems enough to do it. We came 5 or 6 miles last night to better grass. to day we are going to cut hay to take with us, for it is reported we have another desert of 20 miles to cross. at the commencement of the journey that would be thought nothing of, but here it is "some." Emmigrants make a great mistake in calculating upon the load getting lighter. the team get weaker just in proportion.

Wednesday 19th Sepr

The nearer we approach the end of our journey the more tedious and irksome does the journey become. But a fortnight I expect will carry us thro'. "Patience thous rosy lipd cherrub." We are most of us taking the scurvey, myself amongst the rest. the gums bleed and the skin is becoming discoloured in patches, particularly about the legs. I have eaten nothing but bread lately, rejecting fried bacon.— Carson's river is a small stream of good wter about 1 rod wide and 18 inches deep. its margin is marked by aline of cotton woods of large size, lovely to behold to our desert-weary eyes, differing from Marys river which has nothing but willows. for 300 miles down its banks I did not see a tree thicker than my wrist. The weather continues hazy, making the hills or mountains on each side difficult to be seen. On monday night we saw a large notice stuck up by side of the road, informing us the 20 or some said 25 mile desert might be avoided by going about 10 miles round. about 8 miles of the road heavy sand, and then fine grass valeys, besides other information. this was put up by a philantropic Kentuckian, who had been in advance and returned. A leading man of our party observed he was a fool for his pains, tho' he profited by the information. We went that road and found the best grass we had seen for several hundred miles. It has been observed on this road that a man may have travelled to Sante fee and Chiwawa, and yet derive no information necessary for a trip to California. Of this I suppose Mr Turner can bear witness. speaking Turner Mr Garritt of the Planters house Peoria told me that he offered 3000$ to any one that would take his receipted and pay his expenses for this trip, that he had done all that a man could do for the comfort of his passengers, but what can a man do in a desert. he has purchased provissions from the emigrants at an enormous price, that the order passed for reduciing every mans baggage to 75 lbs was from a committee of 12 and not from him, that his own private stores that he had laid in to emeliorate the ruggedness of the route, went in the general wreck. That was the time an Irishman observed when the old Cogniac "watered the plain." Besides the wear and tare both of body and mind that Turner went thro' must have been great. Garett observed he had seen him drop asleep as he stood. With watching thro' the night, as he was in continual fear some of the men would steal his mules, and been harassed during the day, he must have had a hard time of it. Most of the able bodied passengers are leaving some taking it on foot, and some on horseback, so that his loads will be light fro this onward. And I think he will get through.

Sunday Sepr 23

Again it happens for the third time consecutively that we are making hay on the Sunday. Well the Lord will forgive us, I hope. this time we are making it (and I hope it is the last) to carry us thro the dreaded Kanyon. we have now arrived within eight miles of its mouth, and shall go that distance in the cool of this evening, where we shall feed away the hay and start early in the norng. there is no grass fit to cut nearer than this, and no feed for 4 or 5 miles beyond. There are quantities of sand hill cranes and wild geese flying about here, but they are so wild we have not been able to shoot one. Yesterday we passed boiling springs, the hot water gushed up from holes in the ground in several different places, tho' not actually boiling was so hot I could not hold my hand in. they ran into a little brook or slough forming a fine hot bath

Tuesday Sepr 25

Yesterday morng we breakfasted by starlight, and at the earliest dawn of day, started into the Kanyon. our object in this very early start was to get before a many wagons that lay camped near us. for a great part of the road, only one wagon can pass at a time, and if an accident happens to one all those behind are delayed, till it is either repaired or removed. I had seen something I thought of bad roads before, but this capped the climax. He must have had a bold heart and a daring spirit, that first conceived the idea of the possibility of wagons travelling thro' this mountain pass. Imagine a mountain 6 miles thro' at its base cleft in twain, like an immense crack and all the loose rocks and debris thrown together at the bottom, thro' which flows or rather leaks a mountain stream, with here and there patches of scanty soil, bearing lofty pines 4 and 5 ft in diameter amongst these rocks. and sometimes up steep hills loaded wagons had to pass in places where loose cattle could hardly keep their feet. the great difficulty was in steep places and short turns, where only one or two yoke could pull at a time. every man had to put his shoulder to the wheel. here was the place where light loads and strong wheels where [were] appreciated. the way all along was strewn with broken wagons. the wheels had in some places to drop as much as 3 or 4 ft onto solid rock. A pretty severe test to try the strength of a wheel. But we got through safely, and congratulated ourselves so much that we took a "horn" on the strength of it. The six miles occupied about 8 hours. We took a short rest, and travelled about 4 miles further on a good road to grass, where we are now lying. this evening we shall go 4 or 5 more to the last grass, before we ascend the mountain. The scenery in the pass was very sublime. I made 3 sketches, but oweing to my manual exertions being required they were more hasty than I could have wished.

Friday morng 28th

Wednesday morng having to ascend the mountain we started at the earliest dawn. there being no good grass within a mile or two of the wagons, we tied our cattle to the wheels the night before, and started without giving them their breakfast, a circumstance which we regretted afterwards. the road tho' not so long as through the Kanyon was if possible steeper and more difficult, so much so that we had to double teems and take one wagon at a time. and with all our strength, 6 yoke of oxen and not more than 15 hundred in the wagon, we stalled for the first time since leaving the Missouri. we had partly to unload the wagon, and carry up a many articles on our backs. then with the assistance of 3 or 4 fresh drivers with good whips we gained the summit. the other wagon having less loading, was with some difficulty brought up. we now had 5 miles to go into a valley to grass, where we camped. this was a most fatiguing day to men and oxen.— Yesterday [September 27] we did not get of[f] till 9 O'clock, it being thought advisable to feed our oxen well before we started, as we had the second summit to ascend. it is I believe higher than the first, tho' the road is not so rocky, and fewer short turns on it. we doubled teams only for a mile or two, and reached the top about 2 Oclock, where we took a hasty meal amid the snow. the scenery is sublime, vastness being the great feature to express in a picture of it. here on the very summit of the back bone of the American continent, (and the backbone of the Elephant as the emigrants call it) we were favoured with a storm of hail rain and sleet. the wind blew icy cold. overcoats were in demand, altho in the middle of the day,while in the valley below but a few hours before, the sun was so hot, both coats and vests had to come off. to add to our difficulties the lady in our company was taken with the pangs of labour, and we had to descend as quickly as possible over a most rocky road, to the first grass, which we did not reach till an hour after dark. the wagon was near upsetting several times. how she stood the jolting I cannot imagine. I now hastily pitched my tent, which I gave up for her accomadation, and before morning she was delivered of a little girl, without any of those little luxuries, nay without the common necessities usually had on such occasions by the very poorest class, and she an English woman just from London, and moving in a pretty good sphere of life, but through the improvidence of her husband now reduced and penniless. The grass here was exceedingly scanty not picking enough for a mountain goat, and it was our intention to tie them to the wheels till morng and then drive them a mile or two to a little valley where we heard it was better, but while we were eating supper, tho' only left for 10 minutes 12 of them strayed off, and the hills round being covered with lofty pines and huge rocks, and but a scanty moonlight for the sky was clouded, they could no where be found.

I am now left to watch the remaining 5 in the valley above spoken of, having driven them down there early this morning. While all hands are gone to hunt the others. what makes us more anxious is the Indians in these mountains have a bad name for stealing cattle, notices being stuck up on the trees to that effect. An incident occurred yesterday which nearly proved fatal to one of our party. while ascending a rough rocky hill, the jolting of the wagon caused a loaded rifle to get loose and fell out of the back of the wagon. its muzzle struck the shoulder of the owner, who was pushing behind and immediately exploded, the ball passing over his sholder and between the Doctor and I, (who were but a few steps behind) into the ground. Some deaths and several severe wounds have occurred on the trip amongst the companies by keeping rifles loaded and capped in the wagons.

---------------------------- □ ----------------------------

Eleazar Stillman Ingalls, 1850

Ingalls headed west from St. Joseph, Missouri, on May 3, 1850. He traveled via the Sublette Cutoff to the Humboldt Sink, and reached the Carson River on August 6. After resting, he continued along the river before starting the climb up the mountains on August 15. The summit was reached and on August 21 he was in "Hangtown" or Placerville.

July 27th. started at four o'clock, A.M., traveled down the river two miles, then left the river, struck across a desert plain 12 miles to the river; many think this the Great Desert; it is desert enough, but not the Great Desert. This point will be known by a high mountain dividing two valleys. The river runs to the right of this mountain. At noon we had to feed our horses on willows, there being no grass. We got some rushes by swimming the river. We have now got far enough along to begin to have a sight of the Elephant. The river here runs through narrow clay banks like a canal. Passed the grave of a man found in the river; camped at night on a sand bank, put our horses across the river; grass poor. 17 miles.

July 28th. Sunday. Crossed a sand ridge about two miles, and travelled down the bottom about four miles, where we found some grass and camped. Our horses are failing fast. Kit Carson says truly that the Humboldt is the burying ground for horses and oxen. We pass daily great numbers of dead stock at the camping grounds, in the sloughs, and in the river. The river is nothing but horse broth, seasoned with alkali & salt. The appearance of emigrants has sadly changed since we started. Then they were full of life and animation, and the road was enlivened with the song of "I am going to California with my tin pan on my knee." "Oh, California, that's the land for me," but now they crawl along hungry, and spiritless, and if a song is raised at all, it is, "Oh carry me back to Old Virginia, to Old Virginia's shore." Well, they say misery loves company, so we can have some enjoyment after all, for there is plenty of that kind of company. No one seems to know where we are, even those who traveled the route last year, several of whom are along. Last year the road led immediately on the bottom, but this year it is on the sage plains or second level of the river, the bottoms being so swampy that they cannot be crossed. The Mormon guide for this end of the route, is good for nothing. Yesterday was the worst day for dust that we have had. Every body was literally covered with it so that the drivers could not be recognized. 6 miles.

July 29th. Litwiler and Ranaban killed three antelope yesterday. They packed in two of them about eight miles from the mountains. They arrived in camp about 11 o'clock at night. Passed the clay banks, some perpendicular banks on the opposite side of the river about 50 feet high. From this place is a desert, the river running through narrow clay banks, void of vegetation except the Artemesia or wild sage. The road generally follows the plains back from the river, only approaching occasionally for water. We camped about three P.M. and managed to get a little grass for our horses. 15 miles.

July 30th. Started at four A.M.; route similar that of yesterday. We are now in sight of the Pyramid, a lone peak nearly opposite the upper slough of the sink commonly called the meadow. Road touched the river once or twice to-day for water, but no grass, nothing for feed but willows. 16 miles.

July 31st. Started at one o'clock, A.M., struck the river again 10 miles from camp; no grass, only an arid sage desert. From this it is 25 miles to the slough or meadows, and 13 to water, which will be found at some springs in the gully directly opposite the pyramid. We reached the springs about 10 o'clock, A.M., although one of our horses gave out, which delayed us somewhat, and reached the upper end of the slough about noon, where we obtained some rushes and flags for our horses which they devoured greedily after their long fast on willows. The pyramid at a distance resembles an ancient Mexican pyramid, rising by steps. It may be seen for 40 miles up the river, and serves as a beacon, for the slough or meadows. After baiting we continued down the slough about six miles to some passable springs, and to where there is better grass. We found two cities of tents at the slough quite populous. They would do honor to more civilized countries. The road for a few days past has been strewed with dead stock. I counted to-day 120 head of horses, mules and oxen, and got tired of it before night at that. I suppose I passed 50 head more that I did not count. If there is any worse desert ahead than we have found for 70 miles back, I don't know what it may be. I have noticed several dead horses, mules and oxen, by the road side, that had their hams cut out to eat by the starving wretches along the road; for my own part I will eat the lizzards which infest the sage bushes, before I will eat the stock that died from the alkali. The destitution has reached its height now. Hundreds are entirely out of provisions, and there are none who have any to spare, and but very few who have enough to carry them into the mines. Often, almost daily, will some poor starved fellow come up to the wagon and pray us in God's name to give or sell him a crust of bread; some of them asserting that they have eaten no food for two, or even three days. Money is no consideration for food here; no one will sell it for money, but we always give enough to prevent starvation, when thus importuned, although we have not over five day's provision on hand, putting our trust in Providence for the issue to ourselves—for so long as there is game in the mountains we will never starve.

To-day is the first since the third day of June, that we have been out of sight of snow for a whole day; it has been excessively hot, the dust rising in clouds; roads bad, owing to the deep sand. 32 miles.

August 1st. Remained camped to-day, preparing hay for crossing the Desert, which commences 20 miles from the slough or meadow. There is an abundance of grass at this point for all the stock that can ever reach here. We have to wade to get it, then cart it to the channel, and boat it across that in a wagon box. A man with his wife came into the camp last night on foot, packing what little property they had left on a single ox, the sole remaining animal of their team; but I was informed of a worse case than this by some packers, who said they passed a man and his wife about 11 miles back who were on foot, toiling through the hot sand, the man carrying the blankets and other necessaries, and his wife carrying their only child in her arms, having lost all their team.

August 2nd. We still remain at the meadows. A team came in yesterday evening from Sacramento, loaded with provisions. They ask for rice $2.50 per lb.; for flour $2.00; bacon $2.00; whiskey $2.00 per pint, and brandy $3.00 per pint. We killed a cow this evening which we had picked up a few days ago at a camping ground, where she had been left on account of lameness. She was not exactly beef, but she was better eating than dead mules and horses by the road side; we divided her up in the train and among the starving people who are about us, only saving a small amount for ourselves, which we jerked and dried.

August 3rd. We are still lying by. About two miles below our camp are some falls in the river, at which point the meadows terminate. There is no more grass from here until we reach Carson River, about 66 miles.—Some of the teams that left us above Fort Kearney came in to-day, entirely destitute of provisions, and had been so for some days, although they had contrived to starve along somehow. We heard of them before they got here, and saved a little beef for them.

August 4th. Sunday. Broke up camp and started again. We had stopped three days to recruit our horses before taking the desert, and although we have taken the utmost pains with them, they are weaker now than when we stopped. My advice to all is not to make any stop at this point, but push on to Carson River, for there is so much alkali in the water and grass here that your stock will not recruit. There is no water for the next 20 miles fit for stock to drink. We lost one horse to-day from watering beside the road, four miles before we got to the sink. He died in thirty minutes after drinking, in the greatest agony. Two others were much injured, so much so, that we could only get them to the sink with the greatest difficulty. Trimble and Sublet also lost one. Beware of shallow water along here. 20 miles.

August 5th. Reached the Sink last night about sunset. This is a basin about 80 rods wide and half a mile long. It is usually the last water found on the Humboldt, or where it loses itself in the sand, hence its name, but this year the water is so high that it runs down several miles further before it entirely sinks. There is no grass here whatever, nothing but desert. We broke up our wagon to-day and made pack saddles, being convinced of the impossibility of getting our wagon across the desert, since the loss of the horse yesterday and injury to the others. Last night while we were making our supper on coffee and boiled corn, soon after dark, a man came to us and asked for a drink of water. I gave it to him; after drinking he stood looking wistfully at our corn, then asked me if I would take half a dollar for a pint cup full of it. I told him I would not take half a dollar for it, for money was no consideration for food here. He said no more, but turned sorrowfully away, when I stopped him and asked him if he was in distress. He said that he had eaten nothing for two days but a small piece of dried meat which a man gave him. I then told him that I would not take a half dollar for the corn, but that he was welcome to sit down and eat his fill; for although we were nearly out of provisions, we would divide with a man in distress to the last morsel. He stopped the night with us, and took breakfast, and although urged to stop and cross the desert with us to-day, or take some corn with him, he would not do it, but said that he had taxed our hospitality too much already, and left us this morning. His name was Bayell, he belonged in one of the central counties of Illinois, and was a man of standing and influence at home, and a brother of the I.O.O.F. He said he hailed when he came up to our camp, but it was so dark that I did not see his hail, or I should not have put him to the test, to see whether he was really needy or not. Sublet and company, and Williams & Co. left us this morning to cross the desert; we got our pack saddles completed, and took the desert at 2 o'clock, P.M., and traveled all night. Two of our horses gave out, the same that were alkalied, and we left them. About midnight we reached the first wagon road where we found about four acres of wagons left to decay on the desert; this is the first sand ridge; we passed two other wagon yards before morning at similar ridges, besides great numbers along the road, many of them burning. Who will accurately describe this desert at this time? Imagine to yourself a vast plain of sand and clay; the moon riding over you in silent grandeur, just renders visible by her light the distant mountains; the stinted sage, the salt lakes, cheating the thirsty traveler into the belief that water is near; yes, water it is, but poison to the living thing that stops to drink. Train after train drag their tiresome course along, man and beast suffering all the pangs of thirst toil on, feeling, knowing that if the burning sun finds them on the desert in the coming day, their sufferings will be enhanced ten-fold, if worn out with fatigue and thirst they do not faint by the wayside and give up altogether. Burning wagons render still more hideous the solemn march; dead horses line the road, and living ones may be constantly seen, lapping and rolling the empty water casks (which have been cast away) for a drop of water to quench their burning thirst, or standing with drooping heads, waiting for death to relieve them of their tortures, or lying on the sand half buried, unable to rise, yet still trying. The sand hills are reached; then comes a scene of confusion and dismay. Animal after animal drops down. Wagon after wagon is stopped, the strongest animals are taken out of the harness, the most important effects are taken out of the wagon and placed on their backs and all hurry away, leaving behind wagons, property and animals that, too weak to travel, lie and broil in the sun in an agony of thirst until death relieves them of their tortures. The owners hurry on with but one object in view, that of reaching the Carson River before the broiling sun shall reduce them to the same condition. Morning comes, and the light of day presents a scene more horrid than the route of a defeated army; dead stock line the roads, wagons, rifles, tents, clothes, everything but food may be found scattered along the road; here an ox, who standing famished against a wagon bed until nature could do no more, settled back into it and dies; and there a horse kicking out his last gasp in the burning sand, men scattered along the plain and stretched out among the dead stock like corpses, fill out the picture. The desert! you must see it and feel it in an August day, when legions have crossed it before you, to realize it in all its horrors. But heaven save you from the experience.

An incident occurred this evening which shows well of the selfishness of some people on this route. It was soon after dark; we had taken off the packs to rest our horses, and were sitting and lying in the sage bushes beside the road; one of our companions had a few miles back been compelled to leave a horse, which from mistaken feelings of sympathy for the poor animal, he had neglected to kill. While sitting there, a company of packers came along the road, when, although it was so dark that I could not distinguish one animal from another, our friend caught up his rifle, cocked and presented it towards one of them, exclaiming in an angry tone, "Get off that horse, you g-d d-n-d scoundrel, or I'll shoot him down under you." the fellow slid off the horse instantly, when our friend gave him one of the "dog-onit-est" blowings up, as the Missourians say, that one fellow ever got for riding the poor animal after he had given out. It was our friend's horse, who, dark as it was, recognized his faithful animal. the fellow sloped without saying a word in his defence.

August 6th. Morning still finds us dragging our weary steps along on the desert, with nothing near but endless sand hills and beds of clay. Passed Sublett's and Trimbles and Williams's wagons, which they were compelled from loss of stock to leave. Reached the last sand 13 miles from Carson's River, about 10 o'clock, A.M., where we found a water station, and bought some water for our horses at 75 cts. a gallon. We left the pack of one horse here for the station keeper to bring in at night, and the boys went on with the horses, leaving Fuller, who was pretty much done over, and myself, behind. They reached the river about four o'clock, P.M. We were fortunate enough to find some old friends, P. Welch, and T. Ranahan, who had got up a shelter for themselves and oxen, of tents, cloths, and wagon covers, to protect them from the sun. We stayed with them through the heat of the day, and about night started again, but turned off about a mile from the road to visit a small salt lake, where we found a very good spring of fresh water and a sulphur spring. This lake is about three miles from Carson River; its waters are more salt than the most salt brine, and its shores are encrusted with pure salt. Its bed was evidently once the crater of a volcano. We reached the river about 10 o'clock, P.M., but could not find our camp it was so dark, although we found the next day that we had passed directly through it, but the loss of tents, wagons &c., rendered it impossible to distinguish our comrades who were snoring away, wrapped in their blankets. However, after straggling around until towards midnight, we found the tent of some old esteemed friends, Esq. Hoffman & son, who gave us a hearty welcome and a spare blanket, which, (having already filled ourselves with God's beverage from the Carson river,) was to us a perfect elysian. 46 miles.

August 15th. Passed the Mormon station, saw a party of Californians and Mexicans prospecting. There is gold this side of the mountains. Entered the seven mile Kanyon, which begins the real pass of the Sierra Nevada. A branch of the Carson River runs through it, which stream we follow to its head. The Kanyon is a wild, picturesque place, with perpendicular wall of gray granite hundreds of feet high, with lofty pines in the bottoms, and a perfect chaos of granite blocks rent from the walls above. We were compelled to camp in it with nothing for our horses to eat, which somewhat destroyed the romance of the thing; as for eating ourselves, it is so long since we have had anything to eat that we don't trouble ourselves about it. 23 miles.

August 16th. Got out of the Kanyan into the valley, and stopped to bait. Drove about six miles and camped for the night; grass abundant in this valley. J. Ingalls killed a California partridge to-day. It is larger than a partridge in the States, and finely flavored. 8 miles.

August 17th. This morning we had the Nevadas to climb; this is the point which will stop the Pacific Railroad on this route, if anything will do it. This rise is said to be 9000 feet in 13 miles. After climbing the first mountain we descended to a lake, which is the head of one of the branches of the Sacramento. It is the crater of an extinguished volcano. The next mountain, the Snowy Peak, is still worse than the last, although both for most part of the way are as steep as the roof of a house; in climbing it our road lay over the snow, which was 20 feet deep for 80 rods up its side. Having reached the top of the snowy peaks, we took a cut-off, descended about two miles and camped at a small brook where we found good grass. We had the good fortune to shoot three woodchucks (ground-hogs) this evening which, in addition to three lbs. of flour we coaxed out of a Californian, made us feel as rich as the Rothschilds. We have not eaten for the last two weeks (all of us) as much as one man would have eaten if he could have had all that he required, consequently we are living in the greatest luxury and abundance to-night, having all we can eat. It does not take much to make man happy after all; here we have been starving along for the last month, crossing deserts, drinking rotten, alkali or salt water, or deprived entirely, and now we've got to the top of the Nevadas, around our camp fire amid snow drifts, with plenty of good water and three woodchucks for three of us, and we are the happiest mortals alive; we seem to have forgotten that we ever suffered privation. 16 miles.

Artists

Most of the paintings and drawings that are in this book are the works of James F. Wilkins, William Henry Jackson, and J. Goldsborough Bruff. In addition there are some that are drawn by other artists and emigrants. The recent photographs that accompany the early ones were taken by the author on his recent trips along the California Trail.

James F. Wilkins joined an ox wagon company and headed for California with the rest of the argonauts during the gold rush of 1849. He had come to the United States about 1836 from England and first set up shop as a painter in New Orleans and later in St. Louis where he established a reputation as a respected portrait painter. He set out April 25, 1849, from St. Louis on his adventure to the gold diggings. He planned his trip with the sole idea of painting scenes along the trail, and then to return as soon as possible to paint his large moving murals or panoramas, which were a popular style at that time. He reached the diggings in October and by December he was on his return voyage. He made about two hundred watercolor sketches of scenes along the trail. Upon his return, he prepared his panorama and toured parts of the United States with it for a few years. Little information is known about him in the years following his tour, and he died on his farm in Illinois in 1888. Most of his paintings and sketches were not signed and over the years his works have often been attributed to other artists. Even the locations of the scenes have sometimes been incorrectly identified in some publications. Of the approximately two hundred sketches he had when he returned, only about fifty of them are presently known to exist. All of these are from the first half of the journey up through Soda Springs. None are from the Nevada-California section of the trail.

As a result of the work of the eminent historian John McDermott's research in the 1960s approximately fifty drawings were identified as Wilkins'. However, some books published in the 1970s and 1980s still had them improperly identified. Included in the corresponding photographs are some scenes that are specifically located for the first time in a publication. One of the things noticed about Wilkins' paintings was his tendency to make his paintings more compact. This tendency to squeeze the landscape together may have made it more appealing, but it also had the effect of adding height to his subject. This will be obvious when you compare some of his drawings with the photographs of today. In a similar way he tended to make his mountains pointed even when they weren't. Once these two techniques of his were understood, it became much easier to locate most of the specific locations on the California Trail from which his drawings were made. Today his drawings are located at the State Historical Society of Wisconsin.

William Henry Jackson was born in 1843 when the California Trail was just opening. He did not travel on it until 1866 when it was almost past its heyday. Yet, much of the scenery along the trail had not changed much during the twenty some years that had ensued after its opening. Jackson signed on as a bullwacker on an ox freight wagon team and headed west from Nebraska City. Near Ham's Fork he quit his

Winter in S. Nevada
another on snow-shoes, seeking fuel

J. GOLDSBOROUGH BRUFF
Courtesy, The Henry E. Huntington Library and Art Gallery

J. Goldsborough Bruff served as the captain of the "Washington City and California Mining Association" wagon company in 1849. He made many of the drawings and paintings included in this book.

job, but then joined another wagon company and headed down to Salt Lake City. There he joined another company headed to California by way of the Salt Lake-Los Angeles Road, which coincided with part of the Old Spanish Trail. He returned from California in 1867. During his trip he made many sketches that became the basis for his paintings, which were mainly done in the 1930s. He is perhaps best known for his photographic work of the early west, which started in 1869 when he photographed the construction of the Union Pacific Railroad. Then in the 1870s he served as the official photographer for the Hayden Survey of the Territories, and he was instrumental in making

Yellowstone into the first national park. Some of his early photos and those of others were also used as a basis for his later paintings. Jackson's original trail sketches and many of his paintings are now on exhibit in the Jackson Memorial Room of the Oregon Trail Museum at Scotts Bluff National Monument. Still other Jackson paintings are displayed at Harold Warp's Pioneer Museum at Minden, Nebraska.

J. Goldsborough Bruff was the captain of a wagon company from Ohio called the "Washington City and California Mining Association" that headed west for the California diggings in 1849. He had earlier trained at West Point as a civilian cartographer. His company was comprised of seventeen mule-drawn wagons and sixty-six men. This was typical of the gold rush years as the men went off to make their fortunes while the women remained back home. He kept a diary of his journey, and it is perhaps one of the best and certainly longest of all the one written by the forty-niners. Not only did he include the typical comments about the trail, the topography, and his experiences, he also included numerous pencil and pen sketches of scenes and events and even information about graves and tombstones along the trail. His sketches were very accurate and became the basis for his later paintings. It seems even he fell into the pattern of other painters and when going from his pen and pad to his brush and canvas he sometimes tended to exaggerate some features making them look even more dramatic than the sketches showed. Probably the largest collections of his works are located in The Huntington Library and at the Beinecke Rare Book and Manuscript Library, Yale University Library. Many copies of the original pen sketches can also be found in his book, *Gold Rush.*

Bruff returned east and went to work for the government and the topographical engineers. He produced one of the early maps showing the way over the Sierra Nevada by the Lassen Road and also two maps showing the complete emigrant trail across the country.

Travel westward, and see the trail as depicted by the artists, and compare it with the trail today. ■

Maps

Here are the sections of TH Jefferson's *Map of the Emigrant Road* that was published in 1849. There are four sections of the map. The first two cover the eastern half of the route startinng at Independence, Missouri, through the South Pass. Section III starts at the South Pass and continues past Fort Bridger and Salt Lake to the Humboldt River. This route came to be called the Hastings Cutoff. Section IV shows the rest of the trail from the Humboldt River into California via the Truckee route.

There has been some question among historians as to the availability of this map for the emigration of 1849. It does seem that Bruff had a copy of it on his journey, but it is also true that his company was one of the last to leave that year. Jefferson had gone to California in 1846 and was originally part of the Russell Company, which included Bryant, the Reeds, and the Donners.

However, when the company broke up near Fort Laramie, Jefferson moved ahead. At Fort Bridger he met Hastings and became part of the party that was organized under Hastings'

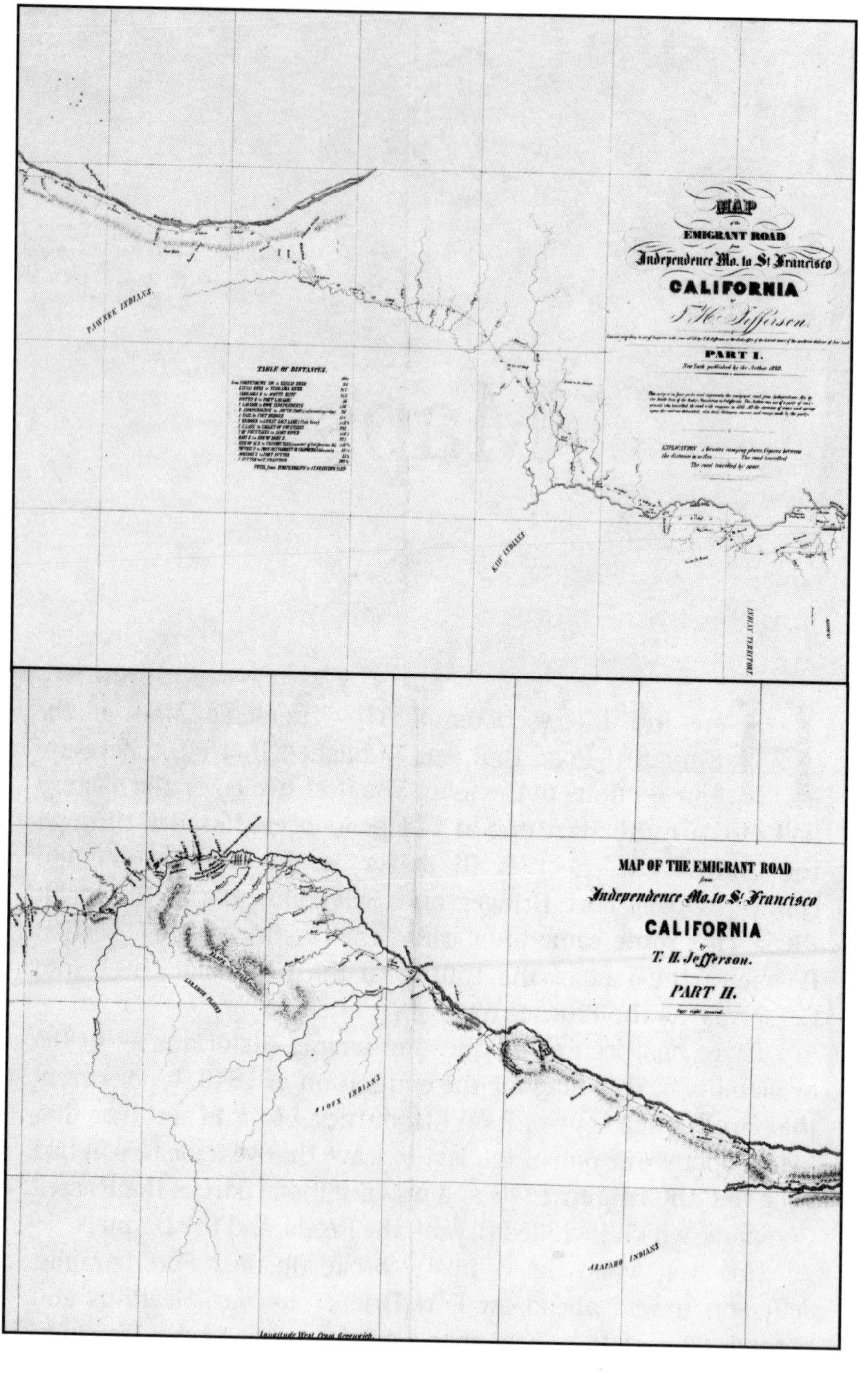

Courtesy, Library of Congress

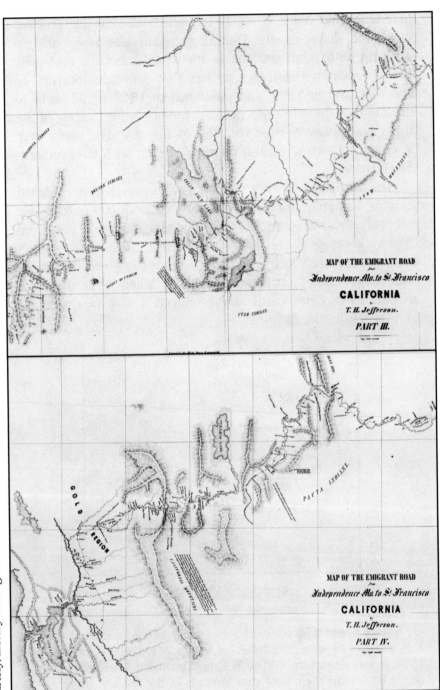

MAP OF THE EMIGRANT ROAD
from
Independence Mo. to S! Francisco
CALIFORNIA
by
T. H. Jefferson.
PART III.

MAP OF THE EMIGRANT ROAD
from
Independence Mo. to S! Francisco
CALIFORNIA
by
T. H. Jefferson.
PART IV.

leadership that made it safely to California over the Truckee route. The slower-moving Donner company was never able to catch up with Hastings, due to their own problems and poor instruction from Hastings. The fact that Jefferson returned to New York and had the map published in 1849 would seem to indicate that the route was not that unreasonable in spite of the earlier bad publicity from the Donner disaster. The maps were based on his own work and records together with the Fremont-Preuss maps.

The last map in this section is the one drawn by Bruff showing Lassen's ranch and his route there. If you look closely you will see the route he took over the Lassen Trail from Lassen's Meadow on the Mary's or Humboldt River. Sutter's Fort would be further south down the Sacramento River off Bruff's map. Also included on it is another trip taken by Bruff in the area in 1850. Later Bruff also produced a map of the whole route to California. ■

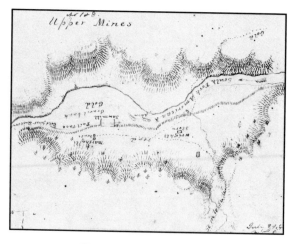

SUTTER'S MILL MAP
Courtesy, National Archives

This is where it all started. Here is a map of the location of Sutter's Mill where gold was discovered by James Marshall on January 24, 1848. It was drawn in July by William Tecumseh Sherman who was only a lieutenant then. Note that North is at the top, but much of the writing is upside down.

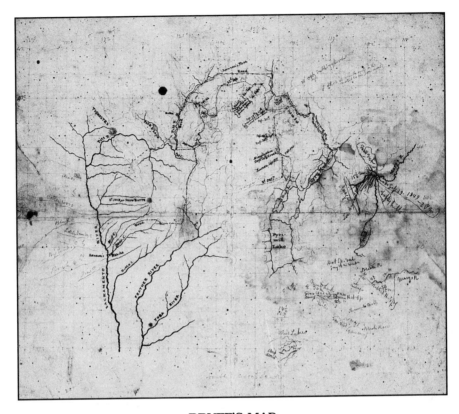

BRUFF'S MAP

Pictorial
Journey

The
California
Trail

MAP AND SITE LOCATIONS

1   Westport Landing
2   Independence Square Area
3   Fort Leavenworth & Weston Area
4   St. Joseph
5   Old Fort Kearny
6   Kanesville & Winter Quarters
7   Alcove Spring
8   Hollenberg Ranch
9   Rock Creek Station
10 Pawnee Village
11 Fort Kearny
12 South Platte Crossing & California Hill
13 Upper Crossing
14 Ash Hollow
15 Courthouse Rock
16 Chimney Rock
17 Scotts Bluff & Robidoux Pass area
18 Hunton Meadows
19 Fort Laramie
20 Register Cliff & Oregon Trail Ruts
21 Laramie Peak
22 Sidley Peak

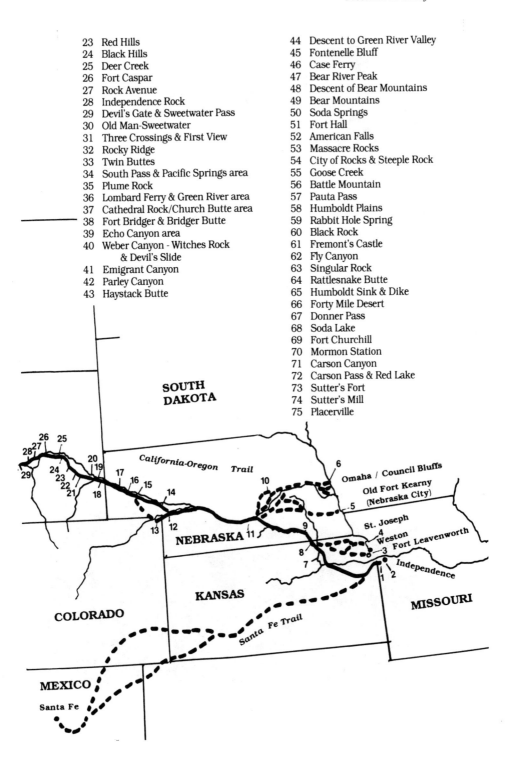

EMIGRANTS NOONING
Courtesy, Museum of New Mexico #3083 by Ben Wittick

Above is an emigrant train nooning on its way west, and below is a recent Oregon-California Trails Association "wagon train" nooning on an expedition on the Hastings Cutoff. Travelers of both yesterday and today welcomed any shade during the heat of the day.

OCTA EXPEDITION TODAY

YOKING THE OXEN
National Park Service

One of the early morning tasks of any wagon company was rounding up the animals and yoking the oxen. This is William Henry Jackson's drawing of it.

Here is a similar scene taking place during the early morning at Rock Creek Station where the oxen are being yoked as part of the living history displays. It is as difficult today as it was in 1866. In addition to the buildings and displays, wagon rides are also available.

YOKING OXEN TODAY

DUST ON THE TRAIL

DIGGING FOR WATER

One of the constant complaints of the emigrants was the dust along the trail. It got into everything. Their eyes burned and they coughed trying to breathe. In July, 1850, Charles W. Smith wrote, "Our road is very dusty. The dust is so light the least wind raises it . . . . Sometimes the dust is so heavy that we cannot see the wagon immediately ahead of us in the train." Even today modern trains have trouble with the dust and become strung out so they do not eat each other's dust.

Water was a major problem along some sections of the trail. Frequently emigrants were forced to dig in the dry riverbeds or ravines hoping to find it. Here is an example of that today at the Dry Sandy. Some of the actual "tanks" dug by the emigrants are still visible there and at other places along the trail.

STORM ON THE PRAIRIE
National Park Service

STORM AT SCOTTS BLUFF ENCAMPMENT TODAY

One of the other frightening experiences for emigrants was the terrible thunderstorms along the Platte. Jackson drew this one based on his own experience while camped near a Mormon train. Emigrants often noted that the rain was so hard their canvas covers and tents were of little real use and everything was soon soaked. Jackson wrote, "The rain beat down so hard it came through the Canvas like a sieve."

The lower picture is part of a living display of a trail re-enactment that was also caught in a thunderstorm at Scotts Bluff.

GRAVE EXCAVATION TODAY

Death was a constant companion for the emigrants. Some historians estimate that there is a grave for every five hundred feet. Here is a grave of a young woman buried at Emigrant Spring on the Slate Creek Cutoff. The grave, which was in danger of being washed away, was recently excavated and relocated by the Oregon-California Trails Association. She appears to have been buried in a coffin made from parts of a wagon box surrounded by a man-made stone vault. Most emigrants were hastily buried, sometimes in the trail itself as a protection against desecration by animals or Indians.

OLD SHOSHONI CAMP
Smithsonian Institution Photo #1667

Most emigrants encountered different Indians along the way. This Shoshoni encampment of Chief Washakie was photographed by Jackson near the South Pass. During the early years most encounters were friendly. However, by the 1850s and then in the 1860s, conditions became much worse, and hostilities became more common. However, in reality accident and disease, not Indians, were the major killers of emigrants along the trail.

Jackson saw Westport Landing more than twenty years after its development as a trailhead or jumping-off place. By then the area had been built up. Here is his vision of what it looked like in its early years.

WESTPORT LANDING
National Park Service

LANDING AREA TODAY

This is a view of the same area painted by Jackson at the junction of the Kansas and Missouri rivers. He would have a hard time recognizing it today. The actual location of Westport Landing is a little further downstream, west of the present ASB bridge. Today a small excursion boat leaves the landing area. This landing was the beginning of modern Kansas City.

INDEPENDENCE SQUARE
Kansas State Historical Society

This well-known drawing of Independence Square shows Independence as many emigrants would have seen it.

Today the courthouse is much larger, and it is said to contain remnants of the earlier courthouses. As in the past, the square is still a hub of activity.

INDEPENDENCE SQUARE TODAY

SPRING PARK

Spring Park is located in Independence. The restored cabin is the Brady Cabin, one of the oldest structures in Independence. It was moved to this location in the 1970s.

NATIONAL FRONTIER TRAILS CENTER TODAY

The National Frontier Trails Center is located in part of the Waggoner-Gates Mill. This was the site of another of the many springs that made Independence famous. The first mill was built on this site in 1847. The center's focus is on the role of Independence as the jumping-off place for all three major trails west, the Santa Fe, Oregon, and California trails.

318 W. Pacific
816-325-7525

FORT LEAVENWORTH LANDING
State Historical Society of Wisconsin, Wilkins

TRAIL RUTS TODAY

Wilkins passed Fort Leavenworth aboard a steamboat on his way to Weston on the east side of the river about May 1, 1849. He may have made this drawing of the landing area while the boat stopped to unload some of its cargo. By the time Wilkins saw it, the fort was already twenty-two years old. Note the blockhouse on the top left where the trail comes up from the river. Part of the blockhouse can still be seen on the top of the hill if you visit the fort today.

The swale going up the hill behind the car corresponds to the trail in Wilkins' painting which goes up the bluff to the blockhouse.

FORT LEAVENWORTH TODAY

ROOKERY TODAY

Here is the landing area today. The river's course has moved away from the bottom of the bluffs, but during heavy rains the area still floods a little. Look closely at the left side of the photo. Two monuments can be seen marking the trail up the bluff. It is the same trail shown in the picture at the left. Note also the very large tree in the photo in front of the brick building to the left of center at the bottom. This could be the same tree behind the unloaded cargo in Wilkins' painting.

Above is the photo of the front of "The Rookery" which was built in 1832 facing the main parade. The rear of the building is shown in Wilkins' painting. The main parade was over the top of the hill near the flag and the main gate in Wilkins' painting.

LANDING AT WESTON
State Historical Society of Wisconsin, Wilkins

Wilkins' painting shows the landing area at Weston when he arrived. Weston was a hub of activity in 1849 and in the 1850s when it served as a jumping-off place.

SEBUS HOUSE TODAY   WESTON TODAY

This is the Sebus house in Weston. It was already standing when Wilkins arrived.

This photo shows the same corner of the town visible in Wilkins' painting. The building to the left is on the bank which led to the river during Wilkins' time. Today Weston is a small town. The river channel has shifted about two miles to the west.

ST. JOSEPH
St. Joseph, Museum

ST. JOSEPH TODAY

St. Joseph, Missouri became another of the jumping-off places for the emigrants heading west. The city was founded by Joseph Robidoux. This 1850 view looks west over the city and across the Missouri River. It also was the starting point for the short-lived Pony Express. Note the domed building to the right in the painting.

Here is a photo showing a similar view of the city today. Note how the city has expanded up the hills blocking the view of the river and how the domed building is barely visible.

OLD FORT KEARNY
State Historical Society of Wisconsin, Wilkins

BLOCKHOUSE REPLICA TODAY

Wilkins crossed the Missouri here at Old Fort Kearny by taking the ferry across it into the Indian territory in Nebraska. Old Fort Kearny was another popular emigrant jumping-off place.

This reproduction of the blockhouse is located today in Nebraska City, the site of Old Fort Kearny.

KANESVILLE CROSSING
National Park Service

Jackson painted this scene of the Kanesville Crossing (Council Bluffs) still further up river with all the wagons lined up waiting for the often unreliable ferries. In 1851 John T. Kerns noted, "On the 10th [May] we tried to get across, but had to give it up as there were too many trains in ahead of us, so we did not get across until the 19th." (That was a real traffic jam!)

OLD MORMON MILL TODAY

This old mill is all that is left of the old Mormon Winter Quarters of 1846-7 which became the site of the Mormon or Upper Ferry, another popular crossing area. The stream that ran the mill is now underground. The town of Florence, today part of Omaha, was built where the Mormons had lived before their journey to Salt Lake under Brigham Young's leadership in 1847. A beautiful Mormon cemetery is on the bluff above and a display area is nearby.

ALCOVE SPRING
National Park Service

This is Jackson's view of Alcove Spring. It is located just above the Independence Crossing of the Big Blue River on the Independence Road in Kansas. Grandma Sarah Keyes, a member of the Donner party, died here on May 29, 1846. She is buried by the present country road near the old parking lot entrance. Her inscription had originally been carved on a large-spreading oak. The actual gravesite is unmarked.

ALCOVE SPRING TODAY

This is a similar view of the alcove. The spring still flows but slowly off on the right side of the photo.

ALCOVE SPRING ROCK TODAY

Here you see the rock with the name Alcove Spring carved on it. On May 30, 1846, Gearge McKinstry carved it after Edwin Bryant named it. Both men were also members of the company that for awhile included the Donners. Unfortunately, it seems that some modern travelers have tried to improve on the original, and some of the letters have been altered a little since the photo was taken.

JFR ROCK CARVING TODAY

Below is the carving of the initials and name of J. F. Reed and the date, May 26, 1846, made when his family camped at Alcove Spring. Reed's family was part of the Donner party. Reed was to play a major role in the story of the infamous Donner tragedy that fateful winter of 1846. Unfortunately even the carving and rock has been damaged since the photo.

HOLLENBERG RANCH TODAY

The Hollenberg Ranch, east of Hanover, was constructed in 1857 right on the trail. It also had the distinction of serving as a Pony Express station from 1860-61. Today it is one of the few standing and unaltered stations.

ROCK CREEK STATION
National Park Service

Twenty miles northwest of the Hollenberg Ranch the trail came to Rock Creek, southeast of present day Fairbury, Nebraska. This Jackson painting seems to be based on a reverse image of an 1859 ambrotype of the East Ranch on the top of the next page.

ROCK CREEK STATION
California State Library, Sacramento, CA

The earliest photo of Rock Creek Station was taken in 1859. The McCanleses built a bridge over the creek near where the early emigrants had forded. The ranch also served as a stage station and Pony Express station.

Today, Rock Creek Station has been reconstructed using the above photo as a model. Note that the building on the far right was not completed at the time the old photo was made, and only the foundation was completed when the present photo was made. The reconstruction should be completed by the mid-90s. Visitors can step back in time and experience life as it was in the 1850s.

ROCK CREEK STATION TODAY

PAWNEE VILLAGE

This deserted Pawnee village along the Platte was painted by Wilkins. The village was seen by many emigrants in 1849. Wilkins passed it on May 31. J. Goldsborough Bruff passed it on June 12 and

PAWNEE LODGE
Smithsonian Institution Photo #1249

State Historical Society of Wisconsin, Wilkins

also commented about it. It was on the road from old Fort Kearny, seventy-five miles east of new Fort Kearny. This is one of Jackson's photographs of a Pawnee village. This could be the village on the Loup River and was similar to the one abandoned shortly before Wilkins and Bruff visited earlier in 1849.

The Pawnee Museum is located in north central Kansas. It was built directly over an excavated site of a large Pawnee lodge. Inside many of the artifacts may be seen just as they were left by the Pawnees.

PAWNEE MUSEUM TODAY

FORT KEARNY

Wilkins made this painting of the new Fort Kearny or Fort Childs, as it was first briefly called. It shows the construction of the fort and is the earliest known illustration dated June 4, 1849.

The fort was much larger when Jackson passed by it in 1866. The fort was about one-half mile from the Platte. As with other military

FORT KEARNY
National Park Service

posts or reservations, emigrants were not supposed to camp on the fort grounds. Some diaries refer to an emigrant register kept there during the California gold rush.

The main parade grounds area with the reconstructed blacksmith shop in the background is shown below.

FORT KEARNY TODAY

O'FALLONS BLUFF

Here is part of the display showing the ruts of the trail as it climbed O'Fallon's Bluff. The trail, which followed close to the Platte River was forced to climb the hill because the river cut right next to the bluffs and left no room for the trail. Modern travelers heading east on I-80 can stop at the rest area and walk along the trail.

Wilkins, it seems, crossed the South Platte on June 13, 1849, in the vicinity of Brule, Nebraska. However, the emigrants crossed the South Platte starting near present-day Hershey, and west along a seventy-five

CROSSING THE SOUTH PLATTE

CALIFORNIA HILL TODAY

mile stretch wherever the best ford could be found. Later, as time passed, the two major fording areas were the Lower Ford near Brule, with the trail pulling up the California Hill, and the Upper Crossing near old Julesberg across from Lodgepole Creek.

This photo shows the swale of the trail near the top of California Hill at the crossing near Brule. The swale is over six feet deep in this section.

State Historical Society of Wisconsin, Wilkins

SOUTH PLATTE CROSSING
National Park Service

SOUTH PLATTE CROSSING AREA TODAY

Jackson's painting shows the upper crossing of the South Platte near Julesburg, Colorado. This was the major route being used when he went west in 1866. It joined the old trail coming up from California Hill and Ash Hollow near Courthouse Rock.

This view shows the South Platte River near where the emigrants crossed. Then there were few if any trees in the valley, and the river was deeper and varied from one half to one mile in width depending on the season and year. Quicksand was a problem for the emigrants crossing the South Platte. Today irrigation has greatly reduced the width and flow of the river.

ASH HOLLOW TODAY

ASH HOLLOW TODAY

On June 15, Wilkins wrote, "Passed to day thro' Ash Hollow, a dry ravine leading to the North Fork, the descent so steep into it that the wagons had to be held back by ropes." Here is the view Wilkins and others had before they started their steep descent. Notice the scars and deep gullies that were caused by thousands of wagons that came down the hill. Now erosion has made them even worse.

Below is a view looking back up the hill. On the top of the hill the swales left by the wagons are very evident as they are cut two or three feet into the ridge line.

COURTHOUSE AND JAIL ROCK
State Historical Society of Wisconsin, Wilkins

On June 19 Wilkins wrote, "Camped tonight in the vicinity of court house rock. This is an immense rock in the shape of buildings standing alone on the prairie, about four miles to the left of the road. Although the distance is so deceptive it does not seem to be more than 1 mile away, and many were the mistakes made by the men in going on foot to see it, most of them turning back after walking a mile or two, apparently getting no nearer. From the point I left the road it must have been six miles. took a sketch of it."

Below is a modern view. Wilkins could have been just off the present highway less than a mile from the entrance to the rocks.

COURTHOUSE AND JAIL ROCK TODAY

CHIMNEY ROCK AND PLATTE RIVER VALLEY
State Historical Society of Wisconsin, Wilkins

On June 19, Wilkins came within sight of Chimney Rock. On the twentieth he made his sketch. Writing on the twenty-first he recorded, "Passed Chimney Rock Yesterday. it is 12 miles from court house. took our noon rest within 1 mile of it. it is a singular formation about 200 feet high, but as I took a sketch of it, I shall not trouble you with a description."

Below is a photo of the same area. Notice how much smaller the chimney looks today. It has eroded and parts have also fallen off since 1849. There are even stories that the military once used it for target practice. Recently lightning struck it and six feet were lost. Even so, part of the difference in height is due to Wilkins' exaggeration and artistic style.

CHIMNEY ROCK AND PLATTE RIVER VALLEY TODAY

SCOTTS BLUFF

This view looking west at Scotts Bluff was taken from Piercy's *Route from Liverpool to Great Salt Lake Valley.* At one time buffalo roamed along the entire Platte Valley from the central plains to the Rocky Mountains.

Today there are still buffalo in the area, but only at the zoo in Scotts Bluff. The farms shown here are slowly being pushed back, and housing developments are now devouring the prairie lands where the buffalo once roamed.

SCOTTS BLUFF TODAY

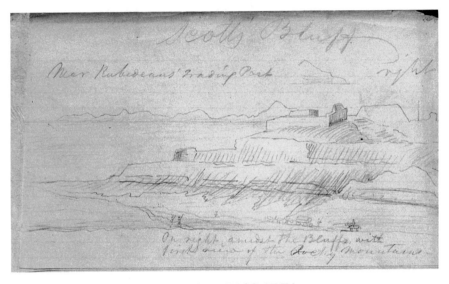

ROBIDOUX PASS AREA
Yale University, Beinecke Rare Book and Manuscript Library

The early trappers and emigrants did not go through Mitchell Pass at Scotts Bluff, but turned a little south of it and traveled through Robidoux Pass. Bruff made this sketch of part of the hills on the north side of the trail as it headed west up the valley to the pass. Below is a view of the same formation today.

ROBIDOUX PASS AREA TODAY

MITCHELL PASS
National Park Service

Mitchell Pass through Scotts Bluff was first used in 1851 and emigrants soon made it the main route replacing the trail through Robidoux Pass. Jackson used the pass in 1866 and camped on the west side of it. Here is one of his paintings looking back at the pass.

Today you can walk along the swale of the trail for more than a mile. The photo shows a similar view.

MITCHELL PASS TODAY

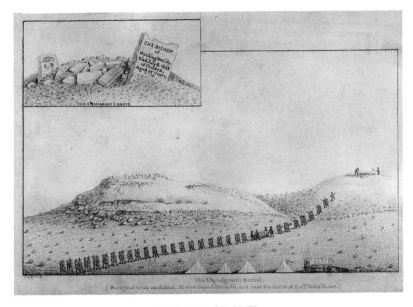

BISHOP GRAVE
The Henry E. Huntington Library and Art Gallery

Bruff made this drawing of a bluff along the North Platte and a funeral procession near where they camped in 1849 on his way to California. It was here that Charles Bishop, a member of his wagon company, died and was buried. His gravesite was only recently located after a search to find the bluff was made by using his drawings of it. The site is near Torrington, Wyoming, by Jamison Bluff in what is known as Hunton Meadows. The grave's location is at the top of the hill at the extreme right in the photo below.

JAMISON BLUFF TODAY

FORT JOHN/LARAMIE
State Historical Society of Wisconsin, Wilkins

Wilkins visited Fort John(Laramie) on June 24, 1849. His view near one of the fords shows the fort well maintained.

The photo below shows only a remnant of the adobe Fort John of 1841. The picture was taken in 1858 when the fort was almost ten years older and falling apart. The army had purchased this "second Fort Laramie" in 1849 and immediately began extensive new construction.

FORT JOHN/LARAMIE
Library of Congress

FORT LARAMIE
National Archives #57-HS-269

This Jackson photo of Fort Laramie was taken from nearly the same spot as the earlier photo, only about twelve years later. Notice the extensive changes in the fort. Old Fort John is gone completely.

The photo below was taken from the exact spot that Jackson used. Notice the growth of trees along the river and its slightly altered course.

FORT LARAMIE TODAY

REGISTER CLIFF TODAY

TRAIL RUTS TODAY

Here is "Register Cliff" where the trail cut close to the bluffs, and upon which the emigrants wrote and carved their names. Note the swale to the right passing the rocks.

Less than a mile further west the trail was forced over the bluffs by the river. Here the wagon wheels cut deeply into the rock, and the route was made clear. This is part of the "Oregon Trail Ruts" display area near Guernsey.

A few days west of Fort Laramie, Wilkins made this drawing of Laramie Peak, the major landmark west of the fort. Some emigrants, however, reported seeing it for the first time from one of the passes near Scotts Bluff.

Below is a photo from near the same location.

LARAMIE PEAK
State Historical Society of Wisconsin, Wilkins

LARAMIE PEAK TODAY

BLACK HILLS
State Historical Society of Wisconsin, Wilkins

Although Wilkins' diary and sketches were usually dated, he sometimes made mistakes with the day and date of the sketches. Sometimes the labeled date was even off by up to ten days. The next three drawings appear to be examples of those cases. The photo below shows Sidley Peak a few miles south of Glendo on I-25 and looks like his drawing above. Using his diary, the date would have put him near Deer Creek, about two days and sixty miles further down the trail. However, the geography of that area doesn't match his drawing.

SIDLEY PEAK TODAY

RED HILLS

State Historical Society of Wisconsin, Wilkins

Wilkins called this "Red Hills." The painting shows the trail as it approached Wagon Hound Creek Crossing, located about nine miles south of Douglas on Highway 94. William Baker called the area "Uncle Sam's brick yard" and said that "there is between 3 and 4 miles of road that is as red as a brick and the hills around are the same color." Based on his date, he would have been back by Courthouse Rock.

Today power lines mar the beauty of the area.

RED HILLS TODAY

BLACK HILLS
State Historical Society of Wisconsin, Wilkins

Another of Wilkins' drawings labeled "Black Hills" is shown above. This name should not be confused with the more famous Black Hills of South Dakota. Here the Black Hills refer to the foothills surrounding Laramie Peak west of Fort Laramie to Deer Creek. The name is appropriate because the many cedar and other trees on the hills give them the appearance of a dark or black color when compared to the lighter grass and sagebrush areas. This painting shows the hills south of the trail and east of LaPrele Creek. Near this spot is the earliest identified grave on the trail. It is of Joel Hembree, a young boy who died on July 19, 1843. He was riding on the wagon tongue, fell off, and was crushed by the wheels. Also near this area is Ayers Natural Bridge.

BLACK HILLS TODAY

FERRY AT NORTH PLATTE

State Historical Society of Wisconsin, Wilkins

Wilkins probably crossed the North Platte a few miles west of Deer Creek. This area around present-day Glenrock was the first crossing area of the North Platte. It was also one of the most dangerous with many drownings being recorded. The last crossing of the North Platte was west of Casper at Red Buttes or Bessemer Bend.

This is one of the ford and ferry sites of the North Platte by Deer Creek. Today the river is narrower and trees cover the riverbanks at the junction of Deer Creek and the North Platte.

NORTH PLATTE CROSSING
AT DEER CREEK TODAY

FORT CASPAR
National Park Service

Here are Jackson's Fort Caspar and the Platte River Bridge and a photo of the reconstructed fort today. The original trading post and bridge were first constructed here in 1858 but burned by the Indians in 1867. Near here was also one of the sites of the Mormon Ferry.

FORT CASPAR TODAY

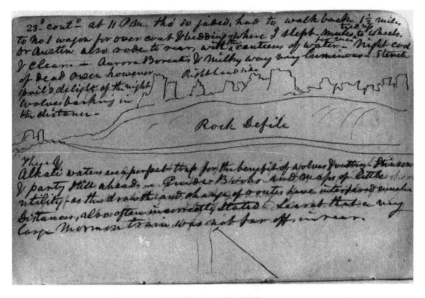

ROCK AVENUE

Yale University, Beinecke Rare Book and Manuscript Library

Bruff made one of the few drawings of Rock Avenue. It is on the trail where it crossed over from the North Platte to the Sweetwater River. Jonas Hittle made another painting; however it was childlike. While you can drive through the avenue, walking it is more rewarding.

ROCK AVENUE TODAY

INDEPENDENCE ROCK
State Historical Society of Wisconsin, Wilkins

Wilkins made this painting of the south side of Independence Rock on July 10, 1849. Note again his tendency to add height to his drawings as is evident when compared with the present photo below.

INDEPENDENCE ROCK TODAY

INDEPENDENCE ROCK
Fort Caspar Museum

He wrote, "it is a solid dome of granite rising out of the prairie, with thousands of names, painted principally with tar." Today one can still see some of the names cut into the rock that Father DeSmet called "The Great Register of the Desert."

This Jackson photo of the rock was taken from the north side. Below is a photo today. Little seems to have changed in this area.

INDEPENDENCE ROCK TODAY

VIEW FROM INDEPENDENCE ROCK
Yale University, Beinecke Rare Book and Manuscript Library

On July 26, 1849, Bruff, like other emigrants, climbed the rock and enjoyed the view. His drawing is looking more to the south when compared to Jackson's photo on the next page.

On June 8, 1850, Charles W. Smith, a former newspaperman on his way to California, wrote, "I climbed up its abruptly rocky sides, and spent a few minutes walking about its summit, though I had not time to examine it as I wished." You also can climb the rock to examine it.

INDEPENDENCE ROCK TODAY

VIEW FROM INDEPENDENCE ROCK
National Archives #57-HS-384

Take your time and be careful. The view is beautiful, but watch your hat; the wind really blows up there.

This Jackson photo above was the basis for one of his paintings of Independence Rock. It shows the view looking back east along the Sweetwater River. Examining the photo below, it seems that only the person is different and the river has meandered a little.

INDEPENDENCE ROCK TODAY

OLD TRAIL AT INDEPENDENCE ROCK
National Archives #57-HS-385

Jackson's photo shows the trail passing the north side of Independence Rock looking back east. The trail shows clearly although its use had dropped greatly by 1870 when the photo was taken.

This is the same view of Independence Rock today. A new interpretive display has been built on the west side right next to one of the many parallel swales of the trail, and it deserves a visit by all modern "emigrants."

INDEPENDENCE ROCK
AND TRAIL VIEW TODAY

PASS IN RATTLESNAKE MOUNTAINS
The Henry E. Huntington Library and Art Gallery

Here is the pass through the Rattlesnake Mountains as Bruff saw it on July 26, 1849, and recorded the 1847 grave with the name Frederick Richard Fulkerson painted on it. Recent investigations have proved that the grave with "T.P.Baker, 1864" carved on the stone really is the grave site of Fulkerson, not Baker. In 1864 Baker used the stone as a place to carve his own name and date, after the original paint had worn off, and then he continued west on his journey.

Below an older highway follows the old trail, but today the highway by-passes it. There is a new interpretive display area where one can look back at both the pass and at Devil's Gate.

RATTLESNAKE PASS TODAY

DEVIL'S GATE

Yale University, Beinecke Rare Book and Manuscript Library

Devil's Gate was a curiosity for the emigrants. Smith said, "Some of our party climbed to the top of the Gate and boasted of having done some daring climbing." Sometimes a few unfortunates fell. Others walked or tried to walk through. Almost all commented about its size.

Jackson's photo was taken from nearly the same place that Bruff used to make his drawing. Another of Bruff's drawings even show similar rocks with a person standing on them.

DEVIL'S GATE

National Archives #57-HS-287

DEVIL'S GATE

State Historical Society of Wisconsin, Wilkins

Wilkins mentioned that "the sides of the gap are so perpendicular . . . they are very high and rugid." He regreted that he "could not pass two or three hours here to finish the sketch of it more highly." His painting above is based on his sketch.

Today it seems that little has changed at Devil's Gate and Jackson would feel right. The feeling of excitement and curiosity experienced by the emigrants can still be felt. The earliest known painting of it was made by Alfred J. Miller in 1837.

DEVIL'S GATE VIEW TODAY

SWEET WATER BUTTES

Wilkins made this panoramic view of the Sweetwater Valley a few miles further up the river. This is the "Old Man" or "Stone Face" as known today, but called Sweet Water Buttes by Wilkins. Split Rock is at the extreme right in the painting.

When Wilkins traveled through here he wrote, "Grass very scarce the camping places, as laid down in the guide books as having plenty of

OLD STONE FACE TODAY

State Historical Society of Wisconsin, Wilkins

grass. we have invariably found none there. it being all eaten off by previous trains." As a result of the conditions, he noted many dead animals and ejected property along the trail in this area. Today the relics are gone, there is more grass, but the ranchers still lose animals along there.

THREE CROSSINGS STATION
National Archives #57-HS-299

This Jackson photo was taken of the abandoned Three Crossings Station. The photo also served as the basis for Jackson's painting of "Three Crossings." The trail actually split near here. One part crossed the river to the north bank, while the other turned away from the river to go around the hill on the left of the photo along what was called the Deep Sand Route on the south side of the river.

Today sagebrush has overgrown the stone piles which served as the foundations for the old station.

THREE CROSSINGS AREA TODAY

TRIBBETTS GRAVE
National Archives #57-HS-246

Above is another Jackson photo of the Three Crossing area showing the grave of a soldier, Bennett Tribbetts, killed in 1862. The grave is on a sand hill a little west of the station site. A marble headstone has replaced the original. The original wooden gravestone shown in the old photo is held by the Fort Caspar Museum.

GRAVE TODAY

THREE CROSSINGS
State Historical Society of Wisconsin, Wilkins

Wilkins took the Three Crossings route and made this drawing of the canyon near where the trail was forced to make its second and third crossings of the Sweetwater. Today the willows have overgrown the riverbanks. The early emigrants would not have found these. Most of them would have been cut.

THREE CROSSINGS TODAY

FIRST VIEW
State Historical Society of Wisconsin, Wilkins

The emigrants who took the trail through Three Crossings got their first view of the Rockies about nine miles west as the trail came back to the Sweetwater for its fifth ford or crossing. Wilkins captured that sight in this painting.

Note once again the artist's "liberties" taken by exaggerating the height of the Wind River Mountains when compared to the photo below in which they are barely visible. However, perhaps it was the excitement Wilkins felt of the first view which made the mountains appear that much bigger to him. I know I certainly was excited when they appeared as the trail crested the hill and began to descend to the Sweetwater.

FIRST VIEW TODAY

This section of the trail was often written about but rarely drawn. This is the Rocky Ridge that caused many a problem for the emigrants. Wilkins painted this view noting in his diary that "the high ridges were rough and rocky, which had we not forded the river several times the day previous and so tightened our wheels, we should very probably have had some breakdowns." Other emigrants were not so lucky.

The early emigrants walked this unless they were very sick. Even today a modern four-by-four has trouble negotiating the rocks, and it is much smoother and quicker to walk.

ROCKY RIDGE
State Historical Society of Wisconsin, Wilkins

ROCKY RIDGE TODAY

This Jackson sketch shows the main trail about one mile after it crossed the Sweetwater for the last time. Some men are hunting antelope. On the horizon were the famous Twin Mounds and far off from the right of the drawing would have been the Wind River Mountains. About eight miles ahead was the great South Pass. When Wilkins was in the same area that year he wrote, "Several of the men went out hunting yesterday, and brought in 3 antelope into camp. this was a great treat, as we have not had any fresh meat for some time. I had some soup made of it this morning which was the first time I had eaten since friday."

Little appears to have changed in the area. Even antelope like those mentioned by Wilkins and shown in Jackson's sketch can be found there.

TWIN BUTTES
Yale University, Beinecke Rare Book and Manuscript Library

TWIN BUTTES TODAY

SOUTH PASS
State Historical Society of Wisconsin, Wilkins

SOUTH PASS TODAY

Wilkins made this painting of South Pass and labeled it that. Jonas Hittle also painted the same scene in 1849. Neither were correct. The pass is actually off to the right of the painting. Their view is a few miles east of the actual pass looking to the left at what appears to be a more natural pass. The real pass was so gradual and indistinct to many emigrants that they wouldn't have recognized it had they not been told they were in it.

PACIFIC SPRINGS
State Historical Society of Wisconsin, Wilkins

The famous Pacific Springs, the first water west of the South Pass, were only about three miles from the summit. Few emigrants stopped at the pass. Many were not aware when they were in the pass, and most wanted to get to the water that ran to the Pacific.

Below is the scene today. Pacific Creek shows up clearly. The springs and ruins of the old Halter and Flick Ranch are to the right just off the photo.

PACIFIC SPRINGS TODAY

This pen sketch by Bruff shows the South Pass area looking back east towards Pacific Springs and the pass.

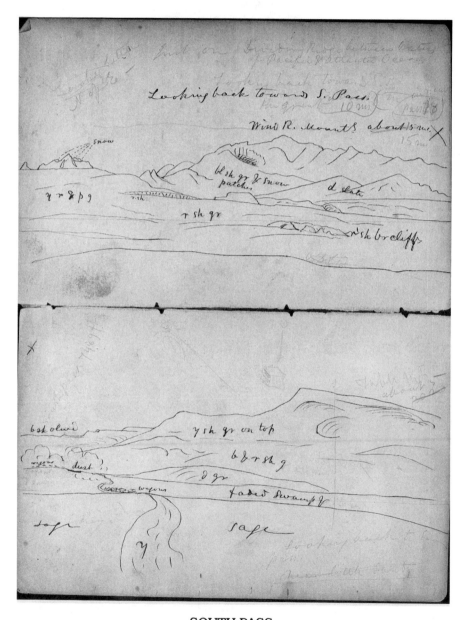

SOUTH PASS

Yale University, Beinecke Rare Book and Manuscript Library

The photos show the same area with the Wind River Mountains on the left.

SOUTH PASS TODAY

SOUTH PASS TODAY

PLUME ROCK

Yale University, Beinecke Rare Book and Manuscript Library

Bruff made this sketch of "Plume Rock" named because of its shape and colors. It is located where the trail turned northwest towards the Dry Sandy Crossing. Describing the same formation, Howard Stansbury wrote on Monday, August 6, 1852, "About a mile from the Dry Sandy, some masses of rock were observed on the right of the road, standing up like pillars; they were found to be composed of coarse sandstone, of an ochery colour. under them were white and red shales, apparently horizontal. The surface of the ground appeared to be the result of the decomposition of the thin ochery rock."

Today the "balanced rock" has been eroded or fallen off, and a hawk nests on the plume.

PLUME ROCK TODAY

WIND RIVER MOUNTAINS
National Park Service

This Jackson painting appears to have been made about a mile past Plume Rock as the trail approaches the crossing of the Dry Sandy. A few miles west of there, the Sublette Cutoff branches off directly west while the old trail continues southwest down to Fort Bridger.

WIND RIVER MOUNTAINS TODAY

Wilkins made this drawing of the trail labeled "Green River Valley." Here is a photo of a similar view where the trail drops down to the flat Green River bottom as it approaches the Lombard Ferry area. However, there is some evidence that indicates this painting might have been labeled incorrectly and that it actually shows the Black Forks River Valley near Fort Bridger, not the Green River Valley.

GREEN RIVER VALLEY
State Historical Society of Wisconsin, Wilkins

GREEN RIVER VALLEY TODAY

FERRY AT GREEN RIVER
State Historical Society of Wisconsin, Wilkins

LOMBARD FERRY AREA TODAY

Wilkins appears to have crossed the Green River down at the Lombard Ferry. Each year the specific location of the ferry may have changed a little with fluctuating river conditions. Today the location is part of a bird sanctuary. A new highway bridge crosses the Green River near the site.

BLUFFS NEAR GREEN RIVER
State Historical Society of Wisconsin, Wilkins

Wilkins made this painting of the bluffs along the Green River a few miles south of the Lombard Ferry Crossing. Coincidently, the site of this painting may also be the site of the Bridger-Fraeb trading post.

GREEN RIVER BLUFFS TODAY

CLAY BLUFFS
State Historical Society of Wisconsin Wilkins

This Wilkins painting labeled "Clay Bluffs," includes the first view of Church Butte or Cathedral Rock which appears as the three small peaks at the far right. The site is from about four and one half miles northeast of the rock or butte. There are only three good vantage points where the Uinta Mountains appear directly behind the "Clay Bluffs" as they do in Wilkins' painting. In the present photo the mountains are barely visible above the bluff. The following page has a close-up view made at the butte.

CLAY BLUFFS TODAY

CATHEDRAL ROCK
State Historical Society of Wisconsin, Wilkins

Cathedral Rock or Church Butte was a noted landmark on the trail to Fort Bridger after crossing the Ham's Fork River. Here is Wilkins' painting labeled "Cathedral Rock" as he saw it on July 24. The photo shows the rock today. It seems either to have eroded some or he "squared" it off to look better.

CHURCH BUTTE TODAY

CHURCH BUTTE
National Archives

Jackson took this photo of Cathedral Rock or Church Butte from a position looking back east at it. Notice that there is a person standing at the base of the rock just to the left of dead center. This view is very similar to another illustration made by Thomas Moran.

Here is Cathedral Rock from the same position, and it shows little erosion. Even the sage looks the same. Note also the person standing by the butte in the photo below.

CHURCH BUTTE TODAY

BRIDGER BUTTE VIEW
National Park Service

Jackson made this sketch looking west towards Fort Bridger and Bridger Butte on July 4, 1867. He was on his return trip from California and a few miles east of the fort.

Below is a photo taken from near the same location a few miles east of Fort Bridger in Urie.

BRIDGER BUTTE TODAY

FORT BRIDGER
State Historical Society of Wisconsin, Wilkins

Wilkins made this painting of Fort Bridger when he camped nearby on July 25. He described it as "merely a few log houses built in a square . . . a few foods are kept for sale here at most exorbitant prices."

This drawing of Fort Bridger is from Stansbury's *An Expedition to the Valley of the Great Salt Lake of Utah.* Bridger Butte is on the far right.

FORT BRIDGER

FORT BRIDGER
National Park Service

When Jackson visited Fort Bridger it was a military post. He never saw the original trading post of Jim Bridger. However, here is his version of the early Fort Bridger. Note its similarity to Stansbury's drawing.

This is a reconstruction of Bridger's original post. Enter the gates and you step back in time to the period of the trappers and the emigrants.

FORT BRIDGER REPLICA TODAY

WAGON TRAIN IN ECHO CANYON
The Church of Jesus Christ of Latter-Day Saints

This well-known photo shows a wagon train winding its way through Echo Canyon. From the amount of water in the creek, it appears to be one of the "out & back" wagon trains leaving Salt Lake City in the spring to pick up Mormon emigrants from back east. The picture was taken looking towards the west with the wagon train heading east on the trail through Echo canyon. The building of the modern Interstate 80 and the earlier building of the railroad altered the position of the stream bed and the original trail. What was once the stream bed is now a marsh area.

ECHO CANYON VIEW TODAY

AMPHITHEATER, ECHO CANYON
National Archives #57-HS-33

The route down Echo Canyon was originally part of the Hastings Cutoff that headed southwest from Fort Bridger. It shortly became part of the Mormon Road or Salt Lake Trail. Jackson took this route on his trip to California. He returned a few years later and took photos along the railroad that was being built. Note that the railroad was constructed parallel to the trail and on top of it in some places.

The photo below shows the "Amphitheater" area today. The modern Interstate 80 has been cut into the other side of the valley at this point. However, the narrow paved road follows the bed of the old dirt trail very closely.

AMPHITHEATER TODAY

GREAT EASTERN, ECHO CANYON
National Archives #57-HS-31

This is Jackson's photo from further down the canyon looking east back up the trail at the "Great Eastern." He also made a painting of the same area.

Below is a photo of the same location today. The old modern highway and railroad that cuts through has flattened the base of the canyon in places. For the emigrants there were some places that were only wide enough for a wagon.

GREAT EASTERN TODAY

JUNCTION OF WEBER AND ECHO CANYON
National Park Service

Jackson's drawing shows the trail as it approached the junction of Echo and Weber canyons.

Here is how the site looks today. Now the interstate, railroad, and earlier highway all run parallel on top of the old trail.

JUNCTION VIEW TODAY

PULPIT ROCK
National Archives #57-HS-29

Pulpit Rock marked the mouth of Echo Canyon. Legend holds that Brigham Young spoke from this rock to his followers on his journey to Salt Lake, but most historians discount this story noting his illness at the time. Jackson made this early photograph showing some of those that did climb Pulpit Rock. Note the changes in the area today. Pulpit Rock was destroyed to make room for the railroad and highway.

PULPIT ROCK AREA TODAY

WITCHES ROCKS
Utah State Historical Society

These odd-shaped rock formations are called Witches Rocks. They are a well-known landmark in Weber Canyon. They were drawn or photographed by a number of people. This drawing of Witches Rocks was made by Albert Tracy in 1859.

Here is the view from the same place. The construction of the earlier highway and the present interstate has cut into the hills, but the view is still the same. The rocks are before Henefer on I-84 a short distance north of the junction with I-80.

WITCHES ROCKS TODAY

DEVIL'S SLIDE

Denver Public Library, Western History Collection

Jackson's photograph shows Devil's Slide in Weber Canyon. The early trail passed this, but after the Donner party cut a new route over the Wasatch Mountains, the Weber Canyon route was used less and less.

Here is Devil's Slide today as seen from I-84 past Henefer.

DEVIL'S SLIDE TODAY

APPROACH TO THE VALLEY OF SALT LAKE
National Park Service

Jackson's painting shows the entrance into the Great Salt Lake Valley.

Below is a photo of Emigration Canyon as the trail came down the mountain to the canyon bottom. This canyon passage was very difficult. It was also part of the route blazed by the Donners.

EMIGRATION CANYON TODAY

PARLEY CANYON
National Park Service

Jackson's painting shows Parley Canyon, the route he traveled down in 1866 and back up in 1867. This route was opened by Parley Pratt in 1850. This became the major route and the parallel route down Emigration Canyon was by-passed.

Today the Interstate 80 follows part of the same route down Parley Canyon into Salt Lake City. Note how the hills in the narrow canyon had to be cut away to make room for the highway.

PARLEY CANYON TODAY

GREEN RIVER FERRY

Returning to the Green River, this painting by Cyrennius Hall is one of the other ferries that developed along the Green River. It appears to be the location of the Case Ferry on the Baker-Davis Cutoff. It is taken from Ghent's *The Road to Oregon*. This cutoff was one of the variants developed to by-pass both the long dip in the old trail to Fort Bridger and also the dry section of the Sublette Cutoff. It rejoins the Slate Creek, Kinney, and Sublette cutoffs.

The photo below shows the area today. An unnamed grave is located near where the photo was taken.

CASE FERRY AREA TODAY

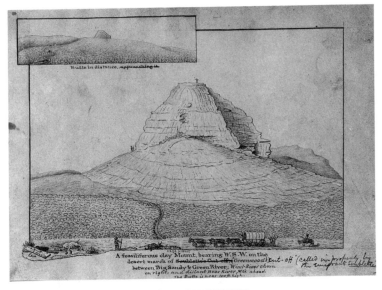

A fossiliferous clay Mount, bearing W. S. W. on the desert march of Sublette's Cut-off, Greenwood's Cut-off (called improperly by the emigrants Sublette) between Big Sandy & Green River; Wind-River chain on right, and distant Bear River Mts ahead. The Butte is near 100 ft high.

HAYSTACK BUTTE

The Henry E. Huntington Library and Art Gallery

On August 4, 1849 Bruff passed this "clay mount" and made his first sketch of it. This painting was made later. This landmark was on the Sublette Cutoff which had separated from the old trail to Fort Bridger a few miles west of the Dry Sandy Crossing.

It seems to look pretty much the same today, only eroded a little more. His painting, unfortunately, made it appear higher than his original more accurate pen drawing. Is located about nine miles north of Farson on US 191.

HAYSTACK BUTTE TODAY

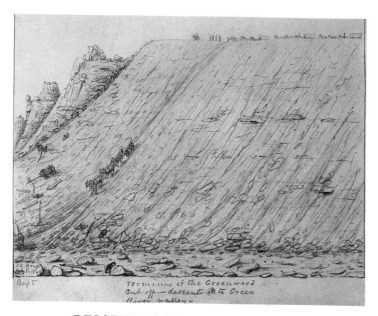

Aug 5.

Terminus of the Greenwood
Cut off – descent into Green
River valley –

DESCENT TO GREEN RIVER VALLEY
The Henry E. Huntington Library and Art Gallery

Bruff made a sketch of the "Descent to the Green" after crossing Sublettes Flat. The drop-off was sharp, and the emigrants descended in a variety of places where they felt safest.

The specific site of Bruff's descent next to the conical rocks remains illusive. Below, however, is one of the other places where the emigrants descended the high tableland. It may not look very steep, but from sitting in the driver's seat, one could not see the trail over the hood for half the descent. You had to "feel" your way down. There is no doubt, it is steep.

DESCENT AT GREEN TODAY

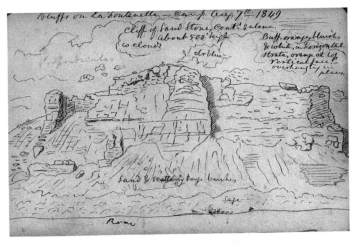

BLUFFS ON FONTENELLE

Yale University, The Beinecke Rare Book and Manuscript Library

Once across the Green River the trail cut southwest up Names Hill, along the river, and then over the high bluffs to Fontenelle's Creek. Fontenelle was an early trapper and trader who had a small cabin on the creek near this bluff. Above is Bruff's sketch of "Fontenelle Bluffs" near the Green.

Below is a photo of the bluff today. It looks the same as it did when Bruff camped there on August 7, 1849. Look closely at Bruff's sketch and you will see a person standing on the top of the bluff, just to the left of center. Look closely at the bottom photo and you will note a person standing there also.

FONTENELLE BLUFF TODAY

BEAR RIVER PEAKS
State Historical Society of Wisconsin, Wilkins

Here we are back on the main trail heading north up the Bear River Valley towards Fort Hall. The Sublette Cutoff and the old trail from Fort Bridger joined near present-day Cokeville. Wilkins made this painting he called "Bear River Peaks" where the trails joined.

Below is a photo taken from Highway 30 as it enters Cokeville. Much of the trail is under or parallels Highway 30 all the way to Soda Springs and Sheep Rock.

SMITH'S FORK VIEW TODAY

DESCENT OF BEAR RIVER MOUNTAINS
State Historical Society of Wisconsin, Wilkins

Wilkins wrote, "Last night we camped along side of the 3rd division of government troops, and this morning we started at sunrise, being obligated to leave the river bottom owing to a cannion (sic), and ascend and descend the mountain the steepest and longest ascent we have made on the route. the government wagons following close behind. I made a sketch of the descent on the other side, but owing to the clouds of dust, it was anything but pleasant to sit sketching." This is the drawing of the descent of the trail after it had climbed the "Big Hill" and descended again into the valley of the Bear River just east of the present town of Dingle Station near the location of Peg Leg Smith's cabin.

Below is a photo of the area today. Note the scars on the mountain where the wagons came down and the farm road at its base.

MOUNTAINS VIEW TODAY

BEAR MOUNTAINS
State Historical Society of Wisconsin, Wilkins

A few days later on August 2 Wilkins camped at present-day Bennington and saw the sunrise and recorded it as "Bear Mountain Sunrise." Baldy is the present name given to the larger mountain to the left of center.

BALDY MOUNTAIN TODAY

BEER (SODA) SPRINGS
State Historical Society of Wisconsin

Below is the present-day Hooper Spring, one of the few soda springs left in the area today. When drinking from some of the springs Wilkins noted that "we took our tin cups and some sugar and drank repeated draughts of excellent soda water." He also said that the water was "impregnated with oxide of Iron." The modern emigrant can also drink from the spring as those earlier ones had done. Use some Tang and you won't notice the taste of iron as much.

Wilkins painted the whole area near Soda Springs. Joel Palmer in 1845 and Chestor Ingersoll in 1847 noted may large white mounds with soda water in them between fifteen and thirty feet tall off to the right of the trail. In 1849 Bryarly wrote extensively about them.

Today the town of Soda Springs has developed in this locale. The cones have been graded away and the Bear River has been dammed. The once famous Steamboat Spring and geyser are now under water. Below is a cone in another city park similar to those seen and climbed by the early emigrants.

HOOPER SPRING TODAY

GEYSER CONE TODAY

Bruff's drawing shows the adobe Fort Hall. When a scene was larger than his paper allowed he drew the rest under it or on the next page and put "X's" where the segments joined.

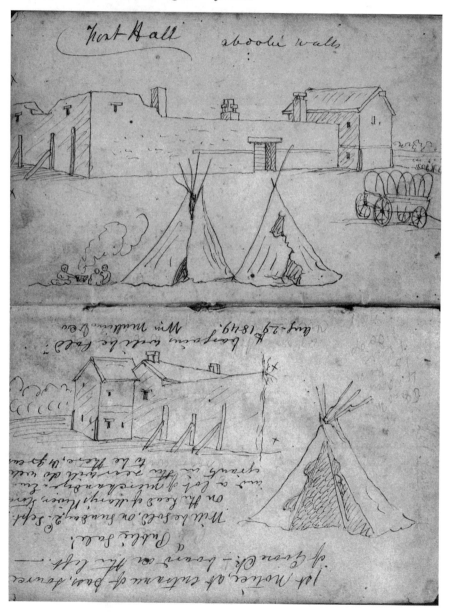

FORT HALL

Yale University, Beinecke Rare Book and Manuscript Library

FORT HALL
National Park Service

Jackson, like many later emigrants, never saw the original Fort Hall. His painting is similar to Bruff's sketch and also to one made by William Henry Tappan.

The replica shown below is located in Ross Park south of Pocatello, Idaho.

FORT HALL REPLICA TODAY

AMERICAN FALLS

Yale University, Beinecke Rare Book and Manuscript Library

Bruff made this drawing of American Falls. The trail was right along the edge of the river. Today the town of American Falls has grown up there. The river has been dammed and the falls harnessed. The view is from near the cemetery.

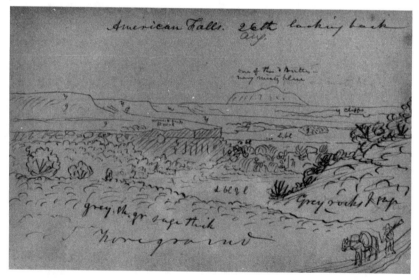

AMERICAN FALLS TODAY

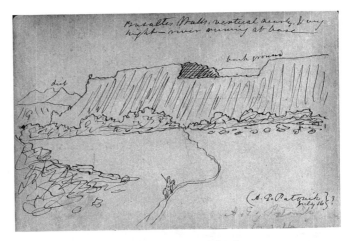

MASSACRE ROCKS

Yale University, Beinecke Rare Book and Manuscript Library

Bruff made this sketch of the trail along the Snake River as it approached the area now called Massacre Rocks. The usage of the present name first appeared in the early 1900s, but it was based on some Indian attacks on emigrant trains in the area in 1862. The passage between the rocks was only wide enough for one wagon when Bruff went through. Over the years highway improvements, including the recent building of the Interstate 15, has widened the opening considerably. In 1849 Bryarly described the area, "The banks of the river here is well marked, being high rocky blufss, resembling those of the beautiful Hudson River. Six miles from Falls, the road passes through two 'Buttes' of solid rock with just space enough for the road."

The view still looks pretty much the same except for the modern interstate. There is also a park in the area.

MASSACRE ROCKS TODAY

CITY OF ROCKS
National Archives #77-KS-44-105

Wilkins, it seems, made many sketches of "City of the Rocks," but none have survived. He was one of the first to use that name for the area. Many emigrants commented on the rocks, and the area was known by many names—Pyramid Valley, Valley of the Rocks, etc.. Some emigrants even painted names on the rocks. One of the larger ones was called "City Hotel" and another "Castle Rock." This photo was taken by Timothy O'Sullivan showing one end of the valley. Below is the same view today. Only the sagebrush and trees have grown some.

CITY OF ROCKS TODAY

Bruff also made many sketches of the rocks. Fortunately his have survived. This sketch was described as "singular formations of disintegrated granite" and on August 29, he rested in a cavelike portion of one he called "Sarcophagus Rock."

CITY OF ROCKS
Yale University, Beinecke Rare Book and Manuscript Library

Here are the two rocks today. Bruff would feel right at home.

CITY OF ROCKS VIEW TODAY

PINNACLE PASS

PINNACLE PASS

Yale University, Beinecke Rare Book and Manuscript Library

Bruff sketched the trail as it headed to Pinnacle Pass where it left City of Rocks. This was another narrow passage with a steep descent on the other side.

PINNACLE PASS TODAY

PINNACLE PASS TODAY

Photos of the area today show how little things have changed. The faint scar of the old trail is just visible in the photo. If you were to walk through the pass, you could see where the wagons left the marks on the rocks.

STEEPLE ROCK
California Historical Society

This famous landmark was called "Steeple Rock" by the emigrants and is referred to as "Twin Sisters" today. It marked the junction of the Salt Lake Road, first blazed by Sam Hensley, and the California Trail coming down from Fort Hall and the Hudspeth's Cutoff. The sketch was made in the 1850s from an early daguerreotype.

The present photo was taken from the same location near the junction of the trails. The immediate area has changed very little. The present road does not come through Pinnacle Pass.

TWIN SISTERS TODAY

GOOSE CREEK
California Historical Society

The next major geographical feature the emigrants had to contend with was Granite Pass. The trail's climb up the mountain was much easier than its steep and twisting descent where the California Trail entered Goose Creek Valley. This is another of the drawings based on early daguerreotypes made of scenes along the trail.

The flat table mountains marked the valley of Goose Creek. Here is an area which is similar to the drawing. After the emigrants traveled up Goose Creek they crossed over the divide into the Humboldt River Basin.

GOOSE CREEK AREA TODAY

Bruff's sketch of Battle Mountain or Shoshone Mesa appears to have been made along the Mary's or Humboldt River near Mosel, Nevada and Argenta Point.

BATTLE MOUNTAIN

Yale University, Beinecke Rare Book and Manuscript Library

Here are the same scenes today. Silver is now mined in these same mountains that the emigrants and 49ers passed on their way to make it rich in the California gold fields. Part of the mountains drawn by Bruff are being excavated.

BATTLE MOUNTAIN TODAY

BATTLE MOUNTAIN TODAY

PAUTA PASS

*Yale University, Beinecke Rare Book
and Manuscript Library*

Bruff made this sketch of Pauta Pass as the trail wound along both sides of the Humboldt or Mary's River. Bruff was on the north side of the river about five miles east of present-day Golconda.

The view today is still the same except that the river bottom is now farmed.

PAUTA PASS TODAY

"THE HUMBUG"

"From all the books that we have read
And all the travelers have said
We most implicitly believed,
Not dreamed that we should be deceived,

That when the mountains we should pass
We'd find on Humboldt fine Blue-grass
Nay that's not all[;] we learned moveover
That we'd get in the midst of clover.

Nay, more yet, these scribing asses
Told of 'other nutricious grasses'
But great indeed was our surprise
To find it all a pack of lies

But when we to the Humboldt came
It soon with us lost all its fame
We viewed it as a great outrage
Instead of grass to find wild sage."

HUMBOLDT PLAINS

To most emigrants the trail along the Humboldt River grew worse and worse as they followed it west and it began to give out or "sink." The rocks, the heat, the dust, and the lack of fresh food took their toll. Many saw only the monotonous plains with the mountains in the distance. Thomas Moran made this drawing of the plains of the Humboldt River. John Grantham wrote "The Humbug" expressing his feeling.

HUMBOLDT PLAINS TODAY

This picture is a similar view of the plains of the Humboldt with mountains in the background. By the time the emigrants reached the present Rye-Patch Reservoir they had to make a decision as to which route to take, the Lassen Route or the main route that continued along the Humboldt until it gave out and then crossed the desert to either the Carson or Truckee river routes.

THE RABBIT-HOLE SPRINGS,
(Wells in a desert.)

RABBIT HOLE SPRING AREA
The Henry E. Huntington Library and Art Gallery

Rabbit Hole Spring was an important watering place on the Applegate-Lassen trail. Like many other springs along the trail, dead and dying animals littered the area. The rotting carcasses often polluted the water. Bruff shows this in his sketch and also commented about the bloating carcasses and those stuck in the watering holes.

Below is the same area today. A spring house covers one of the old springs.

A similar scene to that above is from a different watering hole further east on the trail. Death was always nearby.

RABBIT HOLE SPRING TODAY

DEAD ANIMALS

Mirage

X

very light

dark

dark

very distant

Straw color

Sand nodules & Sage bushes

- y. sh. gr. dead & live Cattle about

BLACK ROCK DESERT
Yale University, Beinecke Rare Book and Manuscript Library

Bruff made this sketch of the Black Rock Desert on the Lassen Road. It was dry and hot, and the only water after crossing the desert could be had at some hot springs at the base of the Black Rock.

Below is the Black Rock Desert. It is still dangerous and desolate even today. Don't travel there alone!

BLACK ROCK AREA TODAY

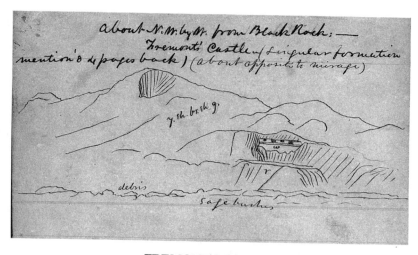

FREMONT'S CASTLE
Yale University, Beinecke Rare Book and Manuscript Library

A little further up the trail on September 23, 1849, Bruff wrote "across the valley to the N. by W. was a very remarkable resemblance of a castle or fortress, of a white substance, (probably clay), in the face of a brownish hill, resting on a shelf of rock, about 1/3 from the plain; This I sketch'd, and named it Fremont's Castle."

Here it is today. Bruff's drawing seems a little more impressive than the real thing.

FREMONT'S CASTLE TODAY

DESCENT TO FLY CANYON

Yale University, Beinecke Rare Book and Manuscript Library

The well-known "Descent to Fly Canyon" was sketched by Bruff on September 25, 1849. He noted the steep descent and the broken wagons littering the canyon floor.

Below is a photo of the area today. Even walking down the hill was difficult. One of Bruff's later paintings of the descent, however, made it appear steeper and deeper than it is. Again, it seems his first sketches were more accurate than many of his later paintings.

CANYON DESCENT TODAY

SINGULAR ROCK

Yale University, Beinecke Rare Book and Manuscript Library

This formation of rock was called "Singular Rock" by Bruff. Below is the same scene today. Little has changed in the area. Only one of the rocks has fallen over, and the trail is overgrown.

SINGULAR ROCK TODAY

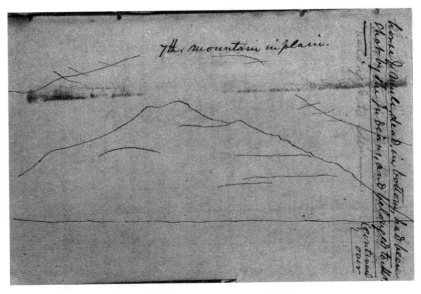

MOUNTAIN ON THE PLAIN

Yale University, Beinecke Rare Book and Manuscript Library

Along the Pit River on the Lassen Route Bruff made this pen drawing of the mountain in the plains. Much of the area still looks the same today. From here the emigrants continued to head south towards Lassen's Peak, then to Lassen's Ranch and, finally, to Sutter's Fort.

RATTLESNAKE/CENTERVILLE BUTTE TODAY

The Applegate-Lassen Route had turned off the main trail along the Humboldt River near the Meadows (Rye Patch Reservoir). Progressing further down the Humboldt as the trail approached the Sink, Randolph Marcy wrote about the route ahead in his 1859 guidebook, "This desert has always been the most difficult part of the journey to California, and more animals have probably been lost here than at any other place. The parts of wagons that are continually met with here shows this most incontestably." That was an understatement. (Remember the conditions encountered and feelings of the emigrants you read about in the diary section.)

FORTY MILE DESERT SIGN

HUMBOLDT (Double) WELLS TODAY

The Forty Mile Desert started after the Sink at the Humboldt Dike. Here the emigrants had to select either the Carson or Truckee Route. No matter which route was selected, part of the Forty Mile Desert had to be crossed. It proved to be as bad, if not worse, than the Black Rock Desert on the Applegate-Lassen Route. There was only one last source of water. Two small wells had been dug a few miles into the desert. These pictured here are the same ones Wilkins mentioned in the diary section. Unfortunately, the water was barely fit for man or beast.

ARTIFACTS TODAY

Even today parts of the wagons, barrel hoops, broken bottles, chains, etc. can still be found in the sands of the Forty Mile Desert. If you do find any, leave them there for the next visitor to see and wonder about the emigrants who were forced to abandon their property in the middle of nowhere.

Here is part of the Truckee Route as it approached the Truckee River. The river, flowing out of the distant mountains, lies a few miles further west from the point where the hills come down to meet the plain. From this point they were still over eight miles away.

FORTY MILE DESERT TODAY

DONNER MONUMENT TODAY

After crossing the desert, one branch of the trail met the Truckee River and more or less followed it up the Sierra Nevada. Here is the monument at Donner Pass State Park near Donner Lake where the Donner party spent their fateful winter. The monument is also the site of the cabin which was occupied by the Breen family of the Donner Party that winter of 1846-7.

This large rock served as a wall for another of the cabins occupied by members of the Donner Party. There is a large marker on it with the names of the Donner party members. These two sites are also mentioned by Bryarly in the diary section. The Donner family spent that winter camped at Alder Creek about six miles further back on the trail.

CABIN ROCK TODAY

SODA LAKE
National Archives #77-KRP-32

Here is one of the salt lakes in the Forty Mile Desert on the Carson Route. Randolph Marcy writes in his 1859 guidebook, "At 9 1/2 miles beyond the mail station, on the desert, a small road turns off from thhe main trace towards a very high sandy ridge, and directly upon the top of the ridge is a salt lake. Upon the extreme north end of this lake will be found a large spring of fresh water, sufficient for 1,000 animals. From thence to 'Ragtown,' on Carson River, is three miles." This spring is also mentioned in the diary section by Ingalls, August 6th. Above is a photo of the salt (soda) lake taken in 1868. Below is a similar photo today.

SODA LAKE TODAY

OLD FORT CHURCHILL

Fort Churchill was built in 1860 on one alternate of the Carson Route that followed the Carson River. The other alternate was more direct but had little water. It was on the other side of the mountains in the background. The photo above is part of a display at the fort showing how it looked after its completion. Today the fort's ruins have been stabilized. The photo below was taken from the point that corresponds to the building in the lower right of the parade grounds in the old drawing above.

FORT CHURCHILL TODAY

MORMON STATION
Nevada Parks Mormon Station

This is the famous Mormon Station that Ingalls mentioned in his diary. It was built around 1850. Many emigrants commented about it in their diaries. This old photo, part of a display, shows how it looked in its later years when it had been altered some.

Below is the reconstruction of the Mormon Station in Genoa. Enjoy a snack or refreshing drink in the cool of the trees or step inside and step back in time.

MORMON STATION REPLICA TODAY

CARSON CANYON
California Historical Society

This drawing shows the trail through the Carson Canyon. Then it was a very difficult passage, narrow and rocky. It was one that the emigrants did not look forward to.

Today the modern road has cut out the twists and turns and most of the river crossings. There are, however, some places along the highway where the old trail can still be found. Walking along them, one wonders how they ever made it. The picture below shows just how rocky the river and canyon floor was.

CARSON CANYON TODAY

CARSON PASS AND RED LAKE
California Historical Society

This old drawing shows the trail as it neared the summit at Carson Pass by Red Lake. The climb had been hard on the emigrants, but in a couple of days they still had another portion of the Sierra Nevada to climb.

This is a similar view today. There is a pull-out and parking area at the summit that has altered the area a little and trees have grown up again that block the view. But you can still walk out and find the emigrants' names, a grave, and the path of the trail that wore deeply into the mountainside.

CARSON PASS AND RED LAKE AREA TODAY

SUTTER'S FORT
Library of Congress

This is Sutter's Fort as it appeared almost a century and a half ago. It was the center of the new empire called "New Helvetia," and it was the goal of most of the early emigrants. Here they found a helpful hand after their long hard journey across the plains, deserts, and mountains.

This is Sutter's Fort as it appears today. Once in the middle of nowhere, it is now surrounded by the city of Sacramento. Only when you walk inside can you get a sense of what it was like many years ago.

SUTTER'S FORT TODAY

SUTTER'S MILL
Bancroft Library

James Marshall, who discovered gold on January 24, 1848, is shown standing in front of Sutter's Mill four years later. By then California had changed more than either Marshall or Sutter would have imagined back in 1848.

Today the mill has been reconstructed near its original location in Coloma, the town that grew up around the site. The river has changed its course a little since the gold rush era and there seems to be more trees.

SUTTER'S MILL REPLICA TODAY

Hangtown Cal

PLACERVILLE
California Historical Society

This is another of the drawings based on early photographs of sites along the trail. This is Placerville, the end of the trail for many gold seekers and also for Betsey and Ike! The tree shown in the drawing near the flagpole in the center of town was the one used for the hanging which gave Placerville its other name—Hangtown!

Below is Placerville today. The town still bustles with activity.

PLACERVILLE VIEW TODAY

Museums
and
Displays

Jefferson National Expansion Memorial, St. Louis, Missouri

Here is the location of the gigantic Gateway Arch, which commemorates St. Louis as the "Gateway to the West." It is located on the site of old St. Louis. Under the arch is the Museum of Westward Expansion. In it can be found exhibits that cover the whole period of westward expansion and development including the California Trail era. It begins with displays of the Lewis and Clark Expedition's exploration of the West and continues with the Indians, trappers, emigrants, cowboys, homesteaders, and railroads until the West was settled and "closed."

The park is located on the west bank of the Mississippi River just off I-55 and I-70, and other points of historical interest are also within walking distance of the memorial park.

Independence, Missouri and Kansas City Vicinity

This area was the beginning of the three major trails west to Santa Fe, Oregon, and California. There are many different museums, historic buildings, and points of interest within the area, which can take a few days to visit and enjoy. Independence Square is often considered to be the starting point for the trails. Here is the present-day courthouse, which contains parts of the early courthouse. Near the square is the National Frontier Trails Center which houses an excellent museum with displays and information about the whole westward journey. It has a fine and rapidly expanding research library. The headquarters of the Oregon-California Trails Association is also located on the site. Spring Park is near the square and contains one of the earliest structures built in Independence, the Brady cabin. Other homes from the trail period are open or in the process of being restored. Some include those of Jack Harris, Alexander Majors, and Archibald Rice-Tremonti. Near the Rice-Tremonti home is the Cave Spring Site in Klein Park. Jim Bridger's grave is located in Mount Washington Cemetery. The Shawnee Methodist Mission in Fairway was a site often visited by early emigrants before they began their trek onto the vast prairies. The Kansas State Historical Society has just finished several years of extensive restoration of this mission. All of these historical landmarks, many well-known to the emigrants, relate to the period of the opening of the trails west.

Fort Leavenworth, Kansas

This is the oldest continuously operated military post west of the Mississippi. It was first constructed in 1827. This area became one of the jumping-off places for the emigrants. On his way to California in 1849 James Wilkins, the artist, drew a picture of this post. Today the post museum, with its emphasis on its military role and the opening of the West to traders and emigrants can be visited; one can also walk on the main parade ground that was the site of early councils with the Indians. At this time, the fort is also the location of the Command and General Staff College for advanced military training.

It is located off Highway 73 just north of present-day Leavenworth, Kansas, which had first been named Douglas City in 1854.

Weston, Missouri

During the early years of the gold rush, Weston was one of the major embarking areas for the emigrants. It was even considered to be one of the greatest port cities of the future. However, due to flooding and a change in the river channel, Weston was left "high and dry" and today is about two miles from the river. The town is presently a Registered Historic District and has a nice museum. In addition there are numerous buildings from its heyday period, and many of the older homes are periodically open to the public. You can stand at the main intersection and also imagine the riverboats pulling up to the area where the railroad tracks now run.

The town is located in Missouri off State Highway 45, a few miles northeast of Leavenworth, Kansas.

St. Joseph, Missouri

Within St. Joseph can be found three nice museums that relate to the period of westward expansion. First, the St. Joseph Museum (11th and Charles Streets) has fine displays that depict the role of the town in the movement west. It also features exhibits about Indians and about the Civil War. The second is the Pony Express Museum (914 Penn Street) with its focus on the history of the Pony Express. The third is the Robidoux Row Museum (Third and Poulin Streets). It is housed in buildings from the 1840s which were built to temporarily house new settlers or emigrants on their westward journey. Its exhibits center on Joseph Robidoux and family and their important role in the West.

Council Bluffs and Omaha Vicinity

This area was another of the jumping-off places for the emigrants, and the principal point of departure for emigrants following the north side of the Platte River. It was also the "Winter Quarters" for the Mormons in 1846-47. The old Mormon Cemetery is located on Thirty-sixth and State Street as is a small visitor center for those interested in the Mormon history of the trail. Nearby is the site of the Mormon Ferry and the old mill, which should be restored. The Joslyn Art Museum (2200 Dodge Street) is also in Omaha and includes excellent exhibits on early Indian life and early expeditions in that area.

Hollenberg Ranch, Hanover, Kansas

A Kansas State Historic Site, this ranch was constructed by Gerat Hollenberg, a German emigrant, who had originally gone west to the gold diggings of California, but left there after not having much success. He came to Kansas in 1857 and made this location his ranch. It was situated on the main California-Oregon Trail west of the junctions of the Independence, St. Joseph, and Fort Leavenworth roads. The structure is unaltered and has a small museum in it. It served as a store for emigrants, a stage station, and later as a Pony Express station. The museum is primarily devoted to its role in the Pony Express venture.

Its location is about one mile east of Hanover on Kansas 243.

Pawnee Indian Village, Kansas

This museum is a Kansas State Historic Site. While it is off the California Trail, it is included because many of the emigrants to California remarked about seeing an old abandoned Pawnee village along the Platte River. James Wilkins' drawing of it is included here as well as a Jackson photograph of a Pawnee village. It is possible that this photo shows the new village, which was established after the older one was abandoned. The museum was constructed over the site of one of the larger lodges of the village, and the floor of the lodge can be viewed with the artifacts left as they were uncovered by the archaeologists. This museum is devoted to showing how the Pawnee Indians lived in this region of northern Kansas and southern Nebraska during the 1800s when the emigrants were traveling through the area.

The museum is run by the Kansas State Historical Society and is located about three miles southwest of Republic, Kansas, about fifty miles west of Hanover.

Rock Creek Station, Nebraska

A Nebraska State Historic Site, Rock Creek Station was first developed in 1857 by SC Glenn who built a small cabin and established a store for the emigrants at the ford of Rock Creek. By 1859, David McCanles purchased the place and established a ranch here, later used as a stage and Pony Express station. At the same time, he built a bridge across Rock Creek. The ranch is perhaps most famous for its role in the Hickok-McCanles shooting of 1861. The Nebraska Game and

Parks Commission has reconstructed both the east and west ranch house complexes to appear as they did in 1859. There is a fine museum, campgrounds, and picnic area. One can also take a short ride in an ox-drawn wagon as the emigrants did. The swale from the thousands of wagons that crossed there are most vivid on the west or north side of the creek.

The park is located about seven miles east of Fairbury off Nebraska Highway 8.

Fort Kearny, Nebraska

This fort is a Nebraska State Historic Park. It originally was called Fort Childs and was constructed in 1848 by Lieutenant Woodbury. Today there is a nice museum that shows the history of the post. The blacksmith shop has been reconstructed along with a stockade. One can walk about the grounds and the main parade and see the locations of some of the other buildings. Some of the large trees standing in the parade area were planted by Lieutenant Woodbury in 1848. Also on the grounds is a reconstructed powder magazine. The area around the fort has changed considerably from the emigrants' era. Then it was dry and sandy; today, with irrigation, it is a rich farming area.

The fort is located south and east of Kearny just west of Nebraska Highway 10.

Nebraska National Trails Museum (Keith County), Nebraska

Plans are presently underway for the long-range development of a major museum and display area near Brule, Nebraska on the banks of the South Platte River. When completed, it will commemorate the historical significance of this whole area. Nearby were the important California Crossing of the South Platte River, the old Beauvais Trading Post, a Pony Express Station, the route of the Union Pacific, and the end of a Texas cattle trail. On the north side of the river is the famous California Hill of the Oregon-California Trail.

California Hill, where the emigrants climbed the plateau after crossing the South Platte, can be visited. It is located four miles west of Brule, Nebraska, on US Highway 30.

Ash Hollow, Nebraska

Today a State Historical Park, Ash Hollow is where the trail dropped back down to the North Platte River valley after crossing the South Platte and the plateau between the two forks of the Platte. At Windlass Hill, one can look at the vivid scars of the trail as it comes down the hill. Also in the park is Ash Hollow Spring. It is here that the emigrants and their animals drank after both crossing the dry plateau between the forks of the Platte and their arduous descent of Windlass Hill. Unfortunately, a nice campground located where the emigrants also used to camp has been eliminated from the park.

Ash Hollow is located on US Highway 26 just before it crosses the North Platte River as the highway approaches Lewellen, Nebraska from the south.

Court House and Chimney Rock, Nebraska

Both Nebraska State Historic Sites, these prominent landmarks on the trail are still a wonder to be seen by the modern traveler. In addition, Chimney Rock holds the dual distinction of also being a National Historic Landmark. A large new interpretive center is being constructed at Chimney Rock that will focus on these two important landmarks and the trail through the Platte River Valley. Chimney Rock was the most recorded landmark of the trails west. The interpretive center will house a wide variety of exhibits with a special emphasis on the emigrants' modes of transportation and what they carried with them. However, it is the view of these landmarks that can still excite the modern traveler, just as it did the emigrant of long ago. As you approach the area, strain you eyes to be the first one to get a glimpse of them just sticking up above the hills—that is the real excitement. For those driving through the area at night, they will experience something the emigrants never did: Chimney Rock is now lit up and can be seen for miles even at night.

Both landmarks are in the vicinity of Bridgeport, Nebraska, off Highway 92. Court House Rock is about five miles south and Chimney Rock about fifteen miles west near Bayard.

Scotts Bluff National Monument, Nebraska

The early emigrants did not pass through Mitchell Pass here at Scotts Bluff, but traveled a few miles south through Robidoux Pass. There are some markers there noting the location of certain historical sites. This was the route used by the early emigrants and forty-niners on their way to California. Information about Robidoux Pass is included in the Oregon Trail Museum.

The trail museum is located in the visitor center at Mitchell Pass. There are living displays there, so you can talk to park attendants playing the roles of emigrants and soldiers. Today, modern emigrants can walk along in the swale of the trail that was opened in 1851 and used heavily after that time. This was also the route later used by the Pony Express and the telegraph. Within the museum itself is one of the finest collections of paintings of scenes along the trail by William Henry Jackson.

Mitchell Pass and the museum are located on Highway 92 just west of Gering.

Fort Laramie, Wyoming

Today Fort Laramie is a National Historic Site and has perhaps the best developed displays and museum along the California-Oregon Trail. It is the pride and joy of the National Park Service. On the grounds are the sutler's store and Old Bedlam, both constructed in 1849. Other buildings have also been restored and are full of interesting displays. Plan on spending a few hours there to take in all the displays and to talk to the sutler, the wives of officers and enlisted men, trappers, cavalrymen, and others who are part of the living displays. Within a few miles of the fort are fine examples of trail ruts and an emigrant grave that can be visited.

The fort is located three miles west of the town of Fort Laramie off US Highway 26.

Register Cliff and Oregon Trail Ruts, Wyoming

These two areas have no museums, but are State Historic Sites. However, both offer the impressive physical evidence of the westward trek. Register Cliff is full of names carved by the emigrants and next to it is a small cemetery. A couple of miles further west is the Oregon Trail Ruts site. This site shows excellent examples of the effects of the thousands of wagons that cut their way west over the hills and rocks. In some places, the wagons cut more than three feet into the hills and the tire and wheel marks are still evident. Here you can walk along the trail ruts and imagine the sights and bellowing sounds of the oxen, wagon wheels, and shouting emigrants as they pulled over these rocky hills.

Both of these are located near Guernsey off US Highway 26.

Wyoming Pioneer Memorial Museum, Douglas, Wyoming

This fine museum covers the Oregon-California Trail period and more. It has something for everyone, including exhibits about pioneer life, ranching, Indians, period costumes, and cartography. It is located on the Douglas County Fairgrounds just inside the main entrance.

Near Douglas are also Ayers Natural Bridge, a site seen by some emigrants, and Fort Fetterman, associated with the Bozeman Trail.

Fort Caspar, Wyoming

Within the city of Casper are some important sites. One is Fort Caspar, which has been reconstructed and has many displays. Near it is the new museum that also houses many displays relating to the emigrant period. Also at the fort is a partial reconstruction of the Guinard Bridge, and one can see some of the remains of the earth and log crib on which the rest of the bridge stood. Also within the town are the sites of the Mormon Ferry established in 1847 and the Reshaw Bridge. Southwest of Casper is another site where the emigrants crossed the North Platte—Bessemer Bend. Today there is a small interpretive display where the emigrants forded the North Platte.

Fort Caspar is located on Fort Caspar Road just before it crosses the North Platte River in the western part of Casper.

Between Fort Caspar and Fort Bridger there are no museums, but there are a number of interpretive sites at major landmarks along the trail and these will be identified. Such landmarks helped to keep the emigrants and trappers heading in the right direction. Interestingly, the city of Casper was named in honor of Lieutenant Caspar Collins, but was misspelled in the process.

Independence Rock, Wyoming

This Wyoming State Historic Site rivals Chimney Rock, Nebraska as claimant to being the most famous of all trail landmarks. Many century-old carvings of the names of emigrants and trappers can still be found on this rock. One can climb the rock as many emigrants surely did. The site is located about fifty miles west of Casper on Wyoming Highway 220.

Devil's Gate, Wyoming

This was a famous landmark and curiosity to the westward emigrant. Many took time to try to either climb to the top or walk through it. Today it is on private grounds, but you can view the area from a new interpretive site about five miles west of Independence Rock on Wyoming Highway 220.

Split Rock, Wyoming

This was another landmark along the trail, and it later became the site of a Pony Express station. The site is located on US Highway 287.

South Pass, Wyoming

This interpretive site is located about four miles west of the actual pass on Highway 28, about forty-five miles southwest of Lander. From it, one can look back east at Pacific Springs and further at the pass itself.

If you are game, you can drive back east from the interpretive site about four and one half miles, turn right on a dirt road at the sign to South Pass, go about three miles, and turn right again on the trail and drive about one mile to the pass itself. Two miles further west over the rough dirt road is the famous Pacific Springs.

Fort Bridger, Wyoming

This was the location of Bridger's and Vasquez's early trading posts. Today it is a State Historic Site. Extensive archaeological work has identified the location of Bridger's trading post and also more of the Mormon's stone fort. There is a fine replica of Bridger's post a short distance from the original site. The museum is fine, and the restoration of many of the remaining buildings is continuing.

It was here at Fort Bridger that the emigrants had to decide whether to go by way of Salt Lake or Fort Hall.

Fort Bridger is located off I-80 in the western part of the town of Fort Bridger.

Pioneer Trail State Park, Utah

This park is on the branch of the trail into Salt Lake City in Emigration Canyon. There is a visitor center and picnic grounds available for the modern traveler. Most of the displays are related to the Mormon migration along this route and the pioneer development of the area. "Old Deseret," a recreated pioneer village, shows life from 1847-69, and it also includes Brighham Young's farmhouse. Here is the Mormon monument, "This Is The Place," commemorating the entrance into the Salt Lake Valley and the Promised Land.

The park is located off Highway 186 at the mouth of Emigration Canyon in the eastern part of Salt Lake City. Within the city are many other sites of historical interest for those concerned with the Mormon migration, and they also deserve the attention of modern travelers.

Soda Springs, Idaho

This was the site of the famous Steamboat Springs and geyser that many emigrants wrote about. Unfortunately, today it is covered by the reservoir and cannot be viewed. Just north of the city of Soda Springs is the famous Hooper Springs. It is located in a city park. One can drink the water there just as emigrants did, but there is no display concerning it. Within the heart of the city is a man-controlled geyser, which is of special interest to the children, and the cone is similar to those the emigrants would have seen and that were painted by Wilkins.

Fort Hall, Idaho

The site of the actual fort is on the Fort Hall Indian Reservation and is identified only by a marker. However, a reproduction of the fort has been built and can be visited. In it are displays from the fur-trapping era and the emigrant period.

The reproduction of Fort Hall can be found at Ross Park and Zoo south of the city of Pocatello off I-15. The children will enjoy roaming through the fort and the zoo.

City of Rocks and Steeple Rock, Almo, Idaho

Through this natural circular valley passed the emigrants who used the Fort Hall and Hudspeth Cutoff. At the southern end of the valley is the famous Steeple Rock or Twin sisters which also marked the junction of the California Trail with the Salt Lake Road. While there is no display in the area, the remnants of the trail can still be seen cutting through the valley. There are also small picnic areas: one in the southern section by Steeple Rock and another in the western section.

City of Rocks is located near Almo, Idaho off Highway 77.

Northeastern Nevada Museum, Nevada

The area around Elko was a camping area for the westward emigrants. A few miles to the south, the Hastings Cutoff joined the main California Trail. The museum primarily focuses on the Indian, pioneer, and mining period of this region. It is certainly worth a visit.

It is located on Business I-80 by the city park in Elko, Nevada.

Rye Patch Reservoir State Recreation Area, Nevada

While there is no major museum or exhibit directed to the California Trail, the trail was on both sides of the Humboldt River in this area. Travelers today can picnic or camp along the Humboldt and look up at the stars at night, much the way emigrants did a century and a half ago. It is northeast of Lovelock, Nevada, located off I-80.

Churchill County Museum, Fallon, Nevada

This is another example of the fine county museums that can be found along the trail. As with others, the focus of this county museum is wider than only the trail period, but that is part of its appeal. The trail is put in its proper perspective. The museum displays relate to the California Trail, Pony Express, Indians, the geological features of the area—there are displays for every interest.

The museum is located in Fallon on Main Street.

Fort Churchill State Historic Monument, Nevada

This fort was built in 1860 on the alternate river route of the Carson Trail at the end of the period considered in this book. It was constructed to protect the emigrants and pioneers in the Carson River Valley. The fort was abandoned in 1869 and sold by 1870. There is a visitor center and interpretive displays related to its military role in the area. The fort is in ruins but one can imagine what it might have been like by walking around the area. Remnants of the trail are still visible in the area. Camping, picnicking, and hiking are available on the grounds.

The fort is located about ten miles south of Silver Springs off US Highway 95 on CR 2B, US Alternate Route 50.

Mormon Station Historic State Monument, Nevada

Here is a replica of the Mormon Station, which was constructed in 1850. It includes a stockade and trading post. Many emigrants stopped here on the Carson route. They were able to rest briefly and obtain needed supplies before their hard pull over the Sierra Nevada. Mormon Station was shortly renamed Genoa by Orson Hyde, an early emigrant, because the area reminded him of the mountains behind Genoa, Italy.

The station is located on SR 57 off I-395 in Genoa, Nevada.

Donner Memorial State Park, California

Here is the monument and museum concerning that fateful winter of 1846 for the Donner party on the Truckee route. They spent that winter in this vicinity. As noted earlier in the history section of this volume, many members of the party were forced into cannibalism in order to survive that dreadful winter. In addition to the visitor center, there are facilities for camping, hiking, fishing, and swimming. You can also drive over to the Alder Creek site where the Donner family and others camped. Donner Pass itself is not located on I-80, but on Donner Pass Road, Highway 40. It is certainly worth the visit. For the hiker in the family, one can follow the Pacific Crest Trail from Donner Pass to Roller Pass and Cold Stream Pass. These were two other passes which took much of the emigrant traffic.

The park is located off I-80 on US Highway 10 near Truckee, California.

Lassen Volcanic National Park, California

Within this park are remnants of the Nobles' Road. This was the cutoff that was opened in 1852. Today you can hike along part of that trail.

Information can be obtained at the visitor centers at the entrances to the park. The park is located on California Highway 89 in northern California, about fifty miles east of Redding.

Sacramento, California

There are two major trail attractions in Sacramento. The first is Sutter's Fort and the second is "Old Sacramento." Sutter's Fort, the center of Sutter's New Helvetia, was the goal of most of the early emigrants and the end of the California Trail. Today, Sutter's Fort has been reconstructed to appear as it did just before the gold rush. The restored central adobe building is the only remaining original structure, the rest having been reconstructed. There are a variety of displays concerning its role in the early history of California. Unfortunately for Sutter, when gold was discovered, it did not bring him wealth as he thought it might, but instead it resulted in the destruction of his empire. The fort is located on Twentieth and L Street in Sacramento.

Sacramento's Old Town or Old Sacramento is well worth the visit. It is the site of two very interesting museums: the Sacramento History Museum (101 I Street), which has an extensive section on the California Trail and gold rush period; and, the Railroad Museum. The whole family will enjoy walking around the old buildings and shops, plus there are many other sites of historic interest in Sacramento which travelers may want to visit.

Marshall Gold Discovery State Historic Park, California

Here is the site of the gold discovery made by Marshall in 1848. A museum and a replica of the mill that was being constructed when the gold was discovered are on the grounds. Marshall is buried in the park. Within the town are other buildings from the gold rush era.

The park is located on California Highway 49 in the town of Coloma, California.

Placerville, California—Historic District

This is one of the many early gold rush towns that developed in 1848–49. it was originally known as "Dry Diggings" but soon became known as "Hangtown" because it was the first gold rush town to use hanging as the method of dealing with lawbreakers. This was the goal of Betsey and Ike of the folksong. Today there are a number of buildings that date from the gold rush era. There are also a number of events related to its early history that would be of interest to the traveler. One is the annual wagon train celebration held in June. It starts out at Lake Tahoe and follows US Highway 50, which closely approximates the Johnson's Cutoff of the Carson route into Placerville.

Placerville is located at the intersection of US 50 and California Highway 49.

The End of the Trail

For any traveler primarily interest in the gold rush era, California Highway 49 from Mariposa in the south to Sierraville in the north traverses the area frequently called the "Mother Lode." Most of the small towns are associated with the gold rush and have buildings from that period. Many have small museums or sites of interest. This area was the goal and "El Dorado" that forty-niners sought.

In addition to the places mentioned, there are numerous highway historical markers and displays along the way or in the rest areas that are not included in this book. The Bureau of Land Management (BLM) has recently begun an extensive program of identifying and marking the trail on BLM lands. Altogether these can provide the modern "emigrant" with information about the trail to California. They usually do not require more than a few minutes stop at each one, but they do add to one's understanding of the trek to California and should be examined. ∎

Additional Reading

There are a variety of books available on the overland or emigrant trails. Every year new books both large and small are becoming available. Because the main California Trail was the same as the Oregon Trail for more than the first half, it gives us a place to begin our investigation into the publications available for your use as a modern emigrant or argonaut along the California Trail.

For the part of the California Trail that coincided with the Oregon Trail there are two very fine books written by Gregory Franzwa. The two books actually supplement each other.

The first is the *Oregon Trail Revisited* and the second is *Maps of the Oregon Trail*. The first takes the reader mile by mile and turn by turn along the modern highways and farm roads that most closely follow the twists and turns of the old emigrant trail. Along with this milepost approach to the trail, there are comments from various emigrants who had taken it themselves. When there are places where the modern traveler might not be able to venture in a passenger car these places are noted. The important historic sites along the way are also mentioned and their significance is explained. While the book does not include all the routes from the jumping-off places, the modern traveler can use this as a guide from Independence, Missouri, and drive along most of the trail all the way past Fort Hall to the Raft River where the California Trail turns off.

The second of his books is perhaps even better for the traveler who reads maps well and can visualize the trip. Again the emphasis is on the main Oregon Trail from Independence, Missouri, so the book is primarily useful for the same section of the California Trail as mentioned above. The trail shows up as a thin red line on his maps. Most of the maps are drawn having a scale of one-half inch to a mile and include not only the main roads but also the farm roads. The book also refers to many of the very important cutoffs, which were not included in his first book. Additionally, his maps are constantly being updated for the most recent discoveries concerning the trail. The location of large segments of visible trail ruts are also located on the maps as are the related historic sites. Therefore, they are much easier for the present-day traveler to find and see.

Another related book is *Historic Sites along the Oregon Trail* by Aubrey Haines. It contains the specific locations of 394 sites of which 318 also apply to the California Trail section. These same sites are also located in Franzwa's book of maps. They include things such as major forts, crossings, locations of graves, landmarks, and even prominent camping grounds with emigrant comments about each place.

Using these three books, located and traveling the first part of the California Trail, is easy and enjoyable.

For a historic overview of the development of the trail and the various jumping-off places mentioned earlier in the book there is Merrill Mattes's book *The Great Platte River Road*. It covers the trails from their various points of origin through the Platte River Valley to Fort Laramie. The book includes a wealth of information and the trail is vividly described by the extensive use of primary source materials.

Another book, which also gives the reader a broad overview of the emigrant experience, is John Unruh's *The Plains Across*. Unlike the other books already mentioned it does not take the reader mile by mile along the trail, but instead discusses the development of the California and Oregon trails over time. It examines the forces that impacted on the trails and their interrelationships. Various topics, such as improvements in the trail, Indians, Mormons, trading posts, the government, emigrant motivations and opinions, are all discussed. This approach coupled with the above book gives the modern traveler an excellent perspective of the trail experienced by the emigrants.

Perhaps the best book for describing the overall historical development of the California Trail is George Stewart's *The California Trail: An Epic with Many Heroes*. This book has just been reprinted and is now available. It covers the development of the trail starting with the Bartleson-Bidwell party in 1841. From that period until the gold rush era, it has a chapter for each year. It mentions the wagon companies for each year and the major ones for the years when travel was heavy. After the gold rush in 1849 the major routes were developed after the trail was established. Stewart spends less time on developments during the 1850s. The book includes many small maps showing the locations of the trails and the various cutoffs with the years of their development. It gives one a good overview of the whole developmental period.

For locating the California Trail where Franzwa's books left off there are a few suggested books. One of the most recently published works is *Emigrant Trails West* by Devere and Helene Helfrich and Thomas Hunt. It is *A Guide to Trail Markers Placed by Trails West, Inc. Along the California, Applegate, Lassen, and Nobles's Emigrant Trails in Idaho, Nevada, and California*. It includes maps of the trail drawn with a scale of four miles to an inch, the specific locations of 201 trail markers, and excerpts from diaries concerning each of the locations. Using the maps it takes the reader from marker to marker starting at the Raft River where the main California Trail leaves the Oregon Trail. It then continues down the main route of the California Trail to where the Applegate Trail turns off, and the Lassen Trail begins. *Emigrant Trails West* also shows where the Nobles' route cuts off from both the Lassen and Applegate trails and follows the California Trail. However, it must be noted that this book does not include the sections for the Truckee and Carson routes that were developed before 1848 nor the Hastings Cutoff.

There is a smaller publication by the Nevada Historical Society called *The Overland Emigrant Trail to California.* It is *A Guide to Trail Markers Placed in Western Nevada and the Sierra Nevada Mountains in California,* which is helpful for the Truckee and Carson trails. The Historical Society has placed fifty-eight markers starting at the point where the Applegate-Lassen trails branch off and then following the trail down the Humboldt to the split in the Carson and Truckee trails. It then follows both up the mountains to the divide, but it unfortunately goes no further. Its two main maps are drawn at a scale of nine miles to an inch and five miles to an inch, which are fairly small. They do include directions to the markers and a description of the markers. However, they do not include excerpts from emigrant diaries for each location.

Charles K. Graydon has written a wonderful short book, *Trail of the First Wagons over the Sierra Nevada.* It covers the Truckee Route west from where it entered California until it approached the Dutch Flats. That section of the trail is then shown on ten maps. Each map has the trail in red and is full of details about the trail.

Another very useful book for covering the trails in Idaho is *Emigrant Trails in Southern Idaho.* The 1976 edition was useful, but the 1993 edition is even better. This later edition was produced by the Bureau of Land Management, Department of the Interior, in cooperation with the Idaho State Historical Society. It includes both the Lander Road and the main trail to Fort Hall, the main trail to Goose Creek, the Hudspeth Cutoff, and the section of the Salt Lake Cutoff that cuts through Idaho. It is an excellent resource with detailed maps, diary excerpts, illustrations, and other useful information about the route. If you are interested in the trail to Oregon through Idaho, this book also covers its main route and the various cutoffs that developed.

In addition to the scholarly approach to the study of the California Trail there are a number of narratives and diaries of emigrants along the trail. Bruff traveled the trail in 1849. His diary and writings are the source of many of the drawings in the pictorial section of this volume. Unfortunately, his journal published as *Gold Rush: Journals, Drawings, and Other Papers* can be found only in libraries. The work published in 1949 was edited by George Read and Ruth Gaines and is excellent. Bruff was the captain of the company and he noted almost "everything." His route took him to Fort Hall and down over the Lassen or "Greenhorn" route to California. Additional information about Bruff is included in the pictorial section.

One of the journals that has recently been published is *The California Gold Rush Overland Diary of Bryon McKinstry*. This was published in 1975 and is still available. It includes both the diary of Bryon McKinstry and also the comments made by his grandson Bruce McKinstry as he tried to relocate and retrace the specific route taken to California by his grandfather. McKinstry went to California by way of the Sublette Cutoff, Fort Hall, and the Carson route. It should also be noted that McKinstry was also in the company that pioneered the route on the northern side of the North Platte west of Fort Laramie and rejoined the main trail west of Deer Creek where many of the other emigrants started crossing over. The book is interesting both for its historical narrative and for the experience of one trying to locate specific sites along the California Trail.

Another of the interesting and recently published books is *Overland to California with the Pioneer Line: The Gold Rush Diary of Bernard J. Reid* edited by Mary Gordon. The Pioneer Line was the first commercial venture to bring emigrants and gold seekers to California. The venture was mentioned a number of times by James Wilkins whose drawings are included in the pictorial section. The book includes not only the diary, but also additional comments made later in life by Bernard Reid. Gordon also included many comments from the diaries of other members of the train, and thus affords the reader a variety of perspectives on this first commercial and problem-filled venture.

These are but a few of the many works that a student of the trail would enjoy. There is a ten volume series called *Covered Wagon Women: Diaries and Letters from the Western Trails 1840–1890* by Arthur H. Clark Publishers. Other publishers such as Ye Galleon Press offer reprints of earlier published works on a limited scale. They have a number of fine reprints available for order. Two older books, which are almost considered classics, are Irene Paden's *The Wake of the Prairie Schooner* and *Prairie Schooner Detours* are still available. She traveled the old trails during the 1930s and describes both her experiences and the trails as they existed then.

Additionally, the journals of the various state and local historical societies are another fine source for diaries and should not be overlooked. The publication of the Oregon-California Trails Association, *The Overland Journal,* published quarterly is another excellent source of material. It even includes information about the present condition of the trail and efforts aimed at its preservation. There are also many books available that focus in on specific topics such as the Donner party, John Sutter, or the gold rush. One other area, which must be mentioned, is the bibliographies of all the books mentioned. They are full of outstanding source materials, which you may find of interest.

Happy Reading! Happy Traveling! ■

Bibliography

Books, Booklets, and Articles

Bryant, William Cullen. *Picturesque America.* Vol. II. NY: D. Appleton & Co., 1874.

Driggs, Howard R. *Westward America.* NY: JB Lippincott, 1942.

Estergreen, M. Morgan. *Kit Carson: A Portrait in Courage.* Norman: University of Oklahoma Press, 1962.

Franzwa, Gregory. *Maps of the Oregon Trail.* Gerald, MO: Patrice Press, 1982.

———. *The Oregon Trail Revisited.* Gerald, MO: Patrice Press, 1972.

Froncek, Thomas. "Winterkill, 1846. The Tragic Journey of the Donner Party." *American Heritage.* December, 1976, Vol. XXVIII, No. 1, pp. 29–42.

Ghent, WJ. *The Road to Oregon, A Chronicle of the Great Emigrant Trail.* NY: Tudor, 1934.

Gilbert, William, et al. *The Trail Blazers.* NY: Time/Life Books, 1973.

Graydon, Charles K. *Trail of the First Wagons Over the Sierra Nevada.* St. Louis, MO: Patrice Press, 1986.

Haines, Aubrey. *Historic Sites along the Oregon Trail.* Gerald, MO: Patrice Press, 1981.

Harris, Earl R. *Courthouse and Jail Rocks.* Nebraska State Historical Society, 1962.

Helfrich, Devere and Helene, and Thomas Hunt. *Emigrant Trails West.* Klamath Falls, OR: Craft Printers, Trails West, Inc. 1984.

Hill, William E. *The Oregon Trail, Yesterday and Today.* Caldwell, ID: The Caxton Printers, Ltd., 1986.

Horn, Houston. *The Pioneers.* NY: Time/Life Books, 1974.

Jackson, Clarence S. *Picture Maker of the Old West, William H. Jackson.* NY: Bonanza Books, 1947.

Jackson, Donald Dale. *Gold Dust*. NY: Alfred A. Knopf, Inc., 1980.

Jackson, Joseph Henry, ed. *Gold Rush Album*. NY: Bonanza Books, 1949.

Jackson, William Henry. *Time Exposure*. NY: GP Putnam's Sons, 1940.

Johnson, Paul C. *Pictorial History of California*. NY: Bonanza Books, 1970.

Lavender, David. *California: A Bicentennial History*. NY: WW Norton & Company, Inc. 1976.

———. *The American Heritage History of the Great West*. NY: Bonanza Books, 1982.

Laxalt, Robert, and others. *Trails West*. Washington, DC: National Geographic Society, 1979.

Lewis, Oscar. *Sutter's Fort: Gateway to the Gold Fields*. Englewood Cliffs, NJ: Prentice Hall, Inc. 1966.

Mattes, Merrill J. *Chimney Rock Nebraska*. Nebraska State Historical Society, 1978.

———. *The Great Platte River Road*. Nebraska State Historical Society, 1969.

———. *Scott's Bluff*. Washington, DC: National Park Service, 1976.

———. "The Council Bluffs Road: The Northern Branch of the Great Platte River Road." *Nebraska History*, Vol. 65 (1984), pp. 179–194.

Mokler, Alfred James. *Fort Caspar*. Casper, WY: Prairie Publishing Co., 1939. Reprint: Mountain States Lithographing Co., 1982.

Moody, Ralph. *The Old Trails West*. NY: TY Crowell Co., 1963.

Paden, Irene D. *The Wake of the Prairie Schooner*. NY: The Macmillan Company, 1947.

Place, Marian T. *Westward on the Oregon Trail*. NY: American heritage Publishing Co., Inc. 1962.

Ross, Marvin C. *The West of Alfred J. Miller*. Norman: University of Oklahoma Press, 1968.

Schlissel, Lillian. *Women's Diaries of the Westward Journey*. NY: Schocken Books, 1982.

Stewart, George R. *The California Trail: An Epic with Many Heroes*. NY: McGraw-Hill Book Co., Inc., 1962.

Troner, Ellen Lloyd, ed. *California, A Chronology and Documentary Handbook*. Dobbs Ferry, NY: Oceana Publications, Inc. 1972.

Unruh, John. *The Plains Across, The Overland Emigrants and the Trans-Mississippi West, 1840–60*. Chicago: University of Illinois Press, 1979.

Wagner, Henry R. *The Plains and the Rockies: A Bibliography of Original Narratives of Travel and Adventure 1800–1865*. Columbus: Long's College Book, Co., 1953.

Wheat, Carl I. *Mapping the Trans-Mississippi West*. Vol. III. San Francisco: Institute of Historical Cartography, 1957.

———. *Emigrant Trails of Southeastern Idaho*. Bureau of Land Management, US Department of the Interior. Idaho, 1979.

———. "The Raft River in Idaho History." *Pacific Northwest Quarterly*. July, 1941. Vol. 32, pp. 289–305.

———. *Story of the Great American West*. Pleasantville, NY: The Reader's Digest Association, Inc., 1977.

———. *Oregon Trail, National Historic Trail*. Comprehensive Management and Use Plan. Appendix II & III. National Park Service. August, 1981.

———. *The Overland Emigrant Trail to California*. Nevada Historical Society.

Diaries, Journals, and Guidebooks

Applegate, Jesse. "A Day with the Cow Column in 1843." *Oregon Historical Quarterly.* Vol I, December 1900, pp. 371–383.

Baker, William. *Diary of William B. Baker—California 1852.* Ventura Historical Museum.

Borthwick, JD. *Three Years in California.* William Blackwood and Sons, 1857.

Bruff, J. Goldsborough. *Gold Rush: Journals, Drawings, and Other Papers.* Edited by Georgia Willis Read and Ruth Gaines. NY: Columbia Press, 1949.

Bryant, Edwin. *What I Saw in California.* NY: D. Appleton and Co., 1849.

Bryarly, Wakeman and Vincent Geiger. *Trail to California. The Overland Journal of Vincent Geiger and Wakeman Bryarly.* Edited by David Potter. New Haven: Yale University Press, 1945.

Burnett, Peter H. "Recollections and Opinions of an Old Pioneer." *Oregon Historical Quarterly.* Vol. V, 1904, pp. 64–99.

Casler, Mel. *A Journal Giving the Incidents of a Journey to California in the Summer of 1859, by the Overland Route.* Fairfield, WA: Ye Galleon Press, 1969.

Child, Andrew. *Overland Route to California.* Milwaukee: Daily Sentinel Steam Power Press, 1852.

Clayton, William. *The Latter-Day Saints' Emigrants' Guide.* St. Louis: Champers & Knapp, 1848. Reprint: Fairfield, WA: Ye Galleon Press, 1981.

Clyman, James. *Journal of a Mountain Man.* Edited by Linda M. Hasselstrom. Missoula: Mountain Press Publishing, 1984.

Dundass, Samuel Rutherford and George Keller. *The Journals of Samuel Rutherford Dundass & George Keller. Crossing the Plains to California in 1849-1850.* Fairfield, WA: Ye Galleon Press, 1983.

Farnham, Elijah Bryan. "From Ohio to California: The Gold Rush Journal of ------." Edited by Merrill J. Mattes. *Indiana Magazine of History,* XLVI (1950), pp. 297–318, 403–420.

Fremont, John Charles. *The Expeditions of J.C. Fremont.* 1 and 2, maps. Edited by Donald Jackson and Mary Lee Spence. Urbana: University of Illinois Press, 1970.

Gordon, Mary. ed. *Overland to California with the Pioneer Line: The Gold Rush Diary of Bernard J. Reid.* Stanford: Stanford University Press, 1983.

Hale, Israel. "Diary of Trip to California." *Society of California Pioneers Quarterly.* Vol. 2, 1925, pp. 61–130.

Hastings, Lansford. *The Emigrants' Guide to Oregon and California.* 1845. Reprint Princeton: Princeton University Press, 1932.

Hittle, Jonas. "Diary, 1849." original (Illinois State Historical Library).

Holmes, Kenneth L. ed. *Covered Wagon Women: Diaries and Letters from the Western Trails 1840-1890.* Glendale, CA: Arthur H. Clark. Vol. I & II, 1983.

Horn, Hosea. *Horn's Overland Guide.* NY: JH Colton, 1853.

Hulin, Lester. *Day Book or Journal of Lester Hulin 1847.* Eugene, OR: Lane County Historical Society, 1960.

Ingalls, Eleazar Stillman. *Journal of a Trip to California by Overland Route Across the Plains in 1850-1.* Fairfield, WA: Ye Galleon Press, 1979.

Ingersoll, Chester. *Overland To California in 1847.* Fairfield, WA: Ye Galleon Press, 1970.

Kerns, John T. "Journal of Crossing the Plains to Oregon in 1852." *Transactions,* OPA, 1914, pp. 148–193.

Leinhard, Heinrich. *From St. Louis to Sutter's Fort, 1846.* Edited by Erwin & Elizabeth Gudde. Norman: University of Oklahoma Press, 1961.

McKinstry, Byron N. *The California Gold Rush Overland Diary of Bryon N. McKinstry.* Edited by Bruce L. McKinstry. Glendale, CA: The Arthur H. Clark Co., 1975.

Marcy, Randolph B. *The Prairie Traveler. A Handbook for Overland Expeditions.* NY: Harper & Bros., 1859.

Paden, Irene. "The Ira J. Willis Guide to the Gold Mines." *California Historical Society Quarterly,* XXXII. 1953, pp. 193–207.

Page, Elizabeth. *Wagons West.* NY: Farra & Rinehart, Inc., 1930. (Diary & Letters of Henry Page, 1849)

Parkman, Francis, Jr. *The California and Oregon Trail.* NY: William L. Allison Co., 18--(1849).

Piercy, Frederick. *Route from Liverpool to Great Salt Lake Valley.* Edited by Fawn M. Brodie. Cambridge: The Belknap Press of Harvard University Press, 1962.

Pleasants, William. *Twice across the Plains—1849 & 1856.* Fairfield, WA: Ye Galleon Press, 1981.

Reading, PB. "Journal of Pierson Barton Reading." *Society of California Pioneers Quarterly.* Vol. 6, 1930, pp. 148–198.

Shively, JM. *Route and Distances to Oregon and California.* WA: W. Greer, Printer, 1846.

Smith, CW. *Journal of a Trip to California—Across the Continent from Weston, Missouri to Weber Creek, California in the Summer of 1850.* Edited by RWG Vail. Fairfield, WA: Ye Galleon Press, 1974.

Snyder, Jacob R. "The Diary of Jacob R. Snyder—1845." *Society of California Pioneers Quarterly.* 1931, Vol. 8, pp. 224–260.

Stansbury, Howard. *An Expedition to the Valley of the Great Salt Lake.* Philadelphia: Lippincott, Grambo, and Co., 1852.

Street, Frank. *Concise Description of the Overland Route.* Cincinnati: RF Edwards & Co., 1851.

Tracy, Albert. "Journal of Captain Albert Tracy." *Utah State Historical Society Quarterly.* Vol. XIII, Nos. 1, 2, 3, 4. 1945. pp. 84–117.

Ware, Joseph. *The Emigrants' Guide to California.* St. Louis: J. Halsall, 1849.

Wilkins, James F. *An Artist on the Overland Trail, The Diary of James F. Wilkins, 1849.* Edited by John F. McDermott. San Marino: The Huntington Library, 1968.

Willis, Ira J. "Best Guide to the Gold Mines, 816 Miles." Great Salt Lake City, 1849.

Woodworth, James. *Diary of James Woodworth across the Plains to California in 1853.* Eugene, OR: Lane County Historical Society, 1972.

Pamphlets

"Chimney Rock," National Park Service, Washington, DC, 1974.

"The Donner Party," Donner Memorial State Park, Department of Parks & Recreation, Sacramento, 1977.

"Fort Bridger," Wyoming Recreation Department, State Archives & Historical Department.

"Fort Caspar Museum," Casper, WY.

"Fort Churchill," Nevada Division of State Parks, *Nevada Magazine.*

"Fort Kearny," Nebraska State Historical Society. Ed. Leaflet No. 7.

"Fort Laramie," National Park Service, Washington, DC.

"Hollenberg Pony Express Station," Kansas State Historical Society, Topeka, KS.

"Marshall Gold Discovery State Historic Park," Department of Parks & Recreation, Sacramento, CA.

"Mormon Station," Nevada Division of State Parks, *Nevada Magazine,* 1979.

"The Oregon Trail," National Park Service, Washington, DC.

"The Oregon Trail," Nebraska Game and Parks Commission.

"Rock Creek Station," Nebraska Game and Parks Commission.

"Route of the Oregon Trail in Idaho," Idaho Historical Society Bicentennial Commission and the Idaho Transportation Department, 1974.

"Salt Lake Sites," Salt Lake Convention & Visitors Bureau, Salt Lake City, UT.

"Scotts Bluff," National Park Service, Washington, DC, 1978.

"Self-Guided Tour of Fort Leavenworth, the Gateway to the West," Fort Leavenworth Historical Society, Fort Leavenworth, KS, 1982.

"Weston, Queen of the Steamboat Days, Old Homes Tour," The Weston Historical Museum, 1972.

Index

About the Author

His address may be in the East, but his heart is in the West.

William E. Hill has been traveling west during the summers for most of his life. Part of his family's roots took hold in Kansas after the Civil War. His family frequently visited and vacationed in the West when Bill was young and it never got out of his system.

He has written two other "Yesterday and Today" books. One is on the Oregon Trail and the other is on the Santa Fe Trail. More recently he has written three educational activity books for children. *Reading, Writing, and Riding Along the Oregon-California Trails* is written for middle through high school students. *Heading West* and *Heading Southwest,* which were co-authored with his wife Jan, are designed for primary grade children, and are about the Oregon-California and Santa Fe trails.

He received his BA in History from the University of Minnesota, his MS in Education, and a CAS in Administration from Hofstra University. Bill is a charter life member and former director of the Oregon-California Trails Association, a member of the Santa Fe Trail Association, and life member of the Kansas, Nebraska, and Wyoming historical societies. He lives in Centereach, NY with his wife Jan, and son Will; he teaches social studies in Commack High School, Commack, NY.